HOW TO
TEACH
YOUR BABY
TO READ

HOW TO TEACH YOUR BABY TO READ

THE
GENTLE
REVOLUTION

Glenn Doman
Janet Doman

The Gentle Revolution Press™

Towson, Maryland

Cover photographer: Stan Schnier, New York
Printer: Kaleido Graphics Services Group, Inc.

Cataloging in Publication Data

Doman, Glenn J.
How to teach your baby to read: the gentle revolution/Glenn Doman,
   Janet Doman — [New ed.].
         p. cm.— (The gentle revolution series)
         Includes index.
         ISBN 1-59117-007-9 (hard)
         ISBN 1-59117-008-7 (soft)

1. Reading (preschool) 2. Early childhood education I. Doman, Janet.
   II. Title. III. Series

Printed in China.

contents

The author wishes to thank the following publishers for their kind permission to quote from copyright material:

Newsweek, Vol. LXI, No. 19 (May 13, 1963), p. 96.

The Bobbs-Merrill Company, Inc., for excerpts from *Natural Education* by Winifred Sackville Stoner, copyright 1914 by The Bobbs-Merrill Company, 1942 by Winifred Stoner Gordon.

Stanford University Press, for excerpts from *The Promise of Youth: Follow-up Studies of a Thousand Gifted Children, Genetic Studies of Genius,* Volume III, by Barbara Stoddard Burks, Dortha Williams Jensen, and Lewis M. Terman (Stanford: Stanford University Press, 1930), pp. 248-50.

Harvard University Press, for brief quotation from Plato's *Republic,* translated by Paul Shorey (the Loeb Classical Library; Harvard University Press), p. 624.

Saturday Review, for brief excerpts from an article by John Ciardi, entitled "When Do They Know Too Much?" (May 11, 1963).

a special word from the authors regarding this third edition

This book first saw the light of day in 1964. It was the very beginning of the Gentle Revolution. Pioneering mothers and fathers embraced the book. Those first parents recognized that this was a real adventure. While Man was just venturing into outer space our parents took the very first steps into inner space—the vast and quite miraculous world of brain growth and development of the tiny child. Those parents knew that tiny children were a great deal more intelligent than most people thought they were. They rolled up their sleeves and got started, and what a wonderful job they have done.

Since that time five million copies have been sold in twenty-two languages, with more on the way. All of the things we said in that original edition seem to be as true today as they were forty years ago.

Only one thing has changed.

Today there are tens of thousands of children, ranging from babies to adults, who learned to read at an early age using this book. As a result, thousands and thousands of mothers have written to us to tell us of the pleasure, joy, and excitement they have experienced in teaching their babies to read. They have related their experiences, their exultation, and occasional frustrations. They have described their victories and their innovations. They have asked a great many penetrating questions. These letters contain a treasure trove of priceless knowledge and splendid insight into tiny children.

They also constitute the greatest body of evidence in the history of the world that proves beyond question that tiny children *can* learn to read, *should* learn to read, *are* learning to read, and, most important of all, *what happens to them* when they go to school and when they grow up.

This precious body of knowledge is what made this new edition not only important but vital to the new generation of parents who have their children's lives as a top priority.

Chapter 7 is changed substantially from the original book—not to change any of the principles laid out earlier, but rather to fine-tune them in light of the vast experience that parents from around the world have had in following these principles.

Chapter 8 is entirely new from the original and details a precise approach to starting a child at each of the significant ages: newborn, infant, tiny baby, baby, and little child.

Chapter 9 is also entirely new and answers the two most commonly asked questions about

teaching babies to read:
1. "What happens to them when they go to school?"
2. "What happens to them when they grow up?"

Here are the answers to these questions from the parents themselves. They do not deal with theoretical children with theoretical problems (so beloved of professionals)—they deal with very real opportunities afforded to very real children by very real and splendid parents.

For the new parent about to join this gentle revolution, welcome.

Go joyously, go like the wind, and enjoy every minute with your child.

There are no chauvinists at The Institutes, either male or female. We love and respect mothers and fathers, baby boys and baby girls. To solve the maddening problem of referring to all human beings as "grown-up male persons" or "tiny female persons," we have referred most often throughout this text to all parents as mothers, and to all children as boys.

Seems fair.

preface

Beginning a project in clinical research is like getting on a train with an unknown destination. It's full of mystery and excitement but you never know whether you'll have a compartment or be going third class, whether the train has a diner or not, whether the trip will cost a dollar or all you've got and, most of all, whether you are going to end up where you intended or in a foreign place you never dreamed of visiting.

When our team members got on this train at the various stations, we were hoping that our destination was better treatment for severely brain-injured children. None of us dreamed that if we achieved that goal, we would stay right on the train till we reached a place where brain-injured children might even be made superior to unhurt children.

The trip has thus far taken a half-century. The accommodations were third class and the diner served mostly sandwiches, night after night, often at three in the morning. The tickets cost all we had, and while some of us did not live long enough to finish the trip none of us would have missed it for anything else the world has to offer. It's been a fascinating trip.

The original passenger list included a brain surgeon, a physiatrist (an M.D. who specializes in physical medicine and rehabilitation), a physical therapist, a speech therapist, a psychologist, an educator, and a nurse. Now there are more than a hundred of us all told, with many additional kinds of specialists.

The little team was formed originally because each of us was individually charged with some phase of the treatment of severely brain-injured children—and each of us individually was failing.

If you are going to choose a creative field in which to work, it is difficult to pick one with more room for improvement than one in which failure has been one hundred percent and success is nonexistent.

When we began our work together over fifty years ago *we had never seen, or heard of, a single brain-injured child who had ever gotten well.*

The group that formed after our individual failures would today be called a rehabilitation team. In those days so long ago, neither of those words were fashionable and we looked upon ourselves as nothing so grand as all that. Perhaps we saw ourselves more practically and more clearly as a group who had banded together, much as a convoy does, hoping that we would be stronger together than we had proved to be separately.

We began by attacking the most basic problem that faced those who dealt with brain-injured children fifty years ago. This problem was *identification*. There were three very different kinds of children with problems who were invariably mixed together as if they were the same. The fact is that they were not even ninety-second cousins. They got lumped together in those days (and, tragically, they still are in much of the world) for the very poor reason that they frequently look, and sometimes act, the same.

The three kinds of children who were constantly put together were deficient children with brains that were qualitatively and quantitatively inferior, psychotic children with physically *normal* brains but unsound minds, and finally truly brain-injured children who had good brains but which had been physically hurt.

We were concerned only with the last type of children, who had suffered injuries to a brain that at conception was perfectly good. We came to learn that although the truly deficient child and the truly psychotic child were comparatively few in number, hundreds of thousands of children were, and are, diagnosed as deficient or psychotic, while they were actually brain-injured children. Generally such mistaken diagnoses came about because many of the brain-injured children incurred injuries to a good brain before they were born.

When we had learned, after many years of work in the operating room and at the bedside, which children were truly brain-injured, we could then begin to attack the problem itself—the injured brain.

We discovered that it mattered very little (except from a research point of view) whether a child had incurred his injury prenatally, at the instant of birth, or postnatally. This was rather like being concerned about whether a child had been hit by an automobile before noon, at noon, or after noon. What really mattered was which part of his brain had been hurt, how much it had been hurt, and what might be done about it.

We discovered further that it mattered very little whether a child's good brain had been hurt as a result of his parents having an incompatible Rh factor, his mother having had an infectious disease such as German measles during the first three months of pregnancy, insufficient oxygen having reached his brain during the prenatal period, or because he had been born prematurely. The brain can also be hurt as a result of protracted labor, by the child's falling on his head at two months of age and suffering blood clots on his brain, by having a high temperature with encephalitis at three years of age, by being struck by an automobile at five years of age, or by any of a hundred other factors.

Again, while this was significant from the research point of view, it was rather like worrying about whether a particular child had been hit by a car or a hammer. The important thing here was which part of the child's brain was hurt, how much it was hurt, and what we were going to do about it.

In those early days, the world that dealt with brain-injured children held the view that the problems of these children might be solved by treating the symptoms which existed in the ears, eyes, nose, mouth, chest, shoulders, elbows, wrist, fingers, hips, knees, ankles, and toes. A large portion of the world still believes this today.

Such an approach did not work then and could not possibly work.

Because of this total lack of success, we concluded that if we were to solve the multiple symptoms of the brain-injured child we would have to attack the source of the problem and approach the human brain itself.

While at first this seemed an impossible or at least monumental task, in the years that followed we and others found both surgical and nonsurgical methods of treating the brain itself.

We held the simple belief that to treat the symptoms of an illness or injury, and to expect the disease to disappear, was unmedical, unscientific, and irrational, and if all these reasons were not enough to make us abandon such an attack, then the simple fact remained that brain-injured children approached in such a manner never got well.

On the contrary, we felt that if we could attack the problem itself, the symptoms would disappear spontaneously to the exact extent of our success in dealing with the injury in the brain itself.

First we tackled the problem from a nonsurgical standpoint. In the years that followed, we became persuaded that if we could hope to succeed with the hurt brain itself we would have to find ways to reproduce in some manner the neurological growth patterns of a well child. This meant understanding how a well child's brain begins, grows, and matures. We studied intently many hundreds of well newborn babies, infants, and children. We studied them very carefully.

As we learned what normal brain growth is and means, we began to find that the simple and long-known basic activities of well children, such as crawling and creeping, are of the greatest possible importance to the brain. We learned that if such activities are denied well children, because of cultural, environmental, or social factors, their potential is severely limited. The potential of brain-injured children is even more affected.

As we learned more about ways to reproduce this normal physical pattern of growing up, we began to see brain-injured children improve— ever so slightly.

It was at about this time that the neurosurgical components of our team began to prove conclusively that the answer lay in the brain itself, by developing successful surgical approaches to it. There were certain types of brain-injured children whose problems were of a progressive nature, and these children had consistently died early. Chief among these were the hydrocephalics, the children with "water on the brain." Such children had huge heads due to the pressure of cerebrospinal fluid that could not be reabsorbed in the normal manner due to their injuries. Nevertheless the fluid continued to be created as in normal people.

No one had ever been quite so foolish as to try to treat the symptoms of this disease by massage or exercise or braces. As the pressure on the brain increased these children had always died. Our neurosurgeon, working with an engineer, developed a tube which carried the excess cerebrospinal fluid *from* the reservoirs called the ventricles, deep inside the human brain, to the jugular vein and thus into the blood stream, where it could be reabsorbed in the normal manner. This tube had within it an ingenious valve that would permit the excess fluid to flow outward while simultaneously preventing the blood from flowing back into the brain.

This almost magical device was surgically implanted within the brain and was called "the V-J shunt." The lives of more than twenty-five thousand children were saved by this simple tube. Many of these children were able to live completely normal lives and go to school with their peers.

This was beautiful evidence of the complete futility of attacking the symptoms of brain injury, as well as the unassailable logic and necessity for treating the hurt brain itself.

Another startling method will serve as an example of the many types of successful brain surgery that are in use today to solve the problems of the brain-injured child.

There are actually two brains, a right brain and a left brain. These two brains are divided right down the middle of the head from front to rear. In well human beings, the right brain (or, if you like, the right half of the brain) is responsible for controlling the left side of the body, while the left half of the brain is responsible for running the right side of the body.

If one half of the brain is hurt to any large degree, the results are catastrophic. The opposite side of the body will be paralyzed, and the child will be severely restricted in all functions. In those days some children had constant, severe, and convulsive seizures which did not respond to any known medication.

It need hardly be said that such children also die.

The ancient cry of those who stood for doing nothing had been chanted over and over for decades. "When a brain cell is dead it is dead and nothing can be done for children with dead brain cells, so don't try." But by 1955 the neurosurgical members of our group were performing an almost unbelievable kind of surgery on such children; it is called hemispherectomy.

Hemispherectomy is precisely what that name implies—the surgical removal of half of the human brain.

At that time we saw children with half a brain in the head and with the other half, billions of brain cells, in a jar at the hospital—dead and gone. But the children were not dead.

Instead we saw children with only half a brain who walked, talked, and went to school like other children. *Several such children were above average, and at least one of them had an I.Q. in the genius area.*

We had long held that, contrary to popular belief, a child might have ten dead brain cells and we would not even know it. Perhaps, we said, he might have a hundred dead brain cells, and we would not be aware of it. Perhaps, we said, even a thousand.

Not in our wildest dreams had we dared to believe that a child might have *billions* of dead brain cells and yet perform almost as well and sometimes even better than an average child.

Now the reader must join us in a speculation. How long could we look at Johnny, who had half his brain removed, and see him perform as well as Billy, who had an intact brain, without asking the question, "What is wrong with *Billy?*" Why did not Billy, who had twice as much brain as Johnny, perform twice as well or at least better?

Having seen this happen over and over again, we began to look with new and questioning eyes at average children.

Were average children doing as well as they might? Here was an important question we had never dreamed of asking.

In the meantime, the nonsurgical members of the team had acquired a great deal more knowledge of how such children grow and how their brains develop. As our knowledge of normality increased, our simple methods for reproducing that normality in brain-injured children kept pace. By now we were beginning to see a small number of brain-injured children reach wellness by the use of the simple nonsurgical methods of treatment which were steadily evolving and improving.

It is not the purpose of this book to detail either the concepts or the methods used to solve the multiple problems of brain-injured children. The book *What To Do About Your Brain-Injured Child* deals with the treatment of the brain-injured child. However, the fact that this is being accomplished daily is of significance in understanding the pathway which led to the knowledge that well children can perform infinitely better than they are doing at present. It is sufficient to say that extremely simple techniques were devised to reproduce, in brain-injured children, the patterns of normal development.

Soon we began to see severely brain-injured children whose performance rivaled that of children who had not suffered a brain injury.

As these techniques improved even more, we began to see brain-injured children emerge who could not only perform as well as average children but, indeed, who could not be distinguished from them.

As our understanding of neurological growth and normality began to assume a really clear pattern, and as methods for the recapitulation of normality multiplied, *we even began to see some brain-injured children who performed at above-average, or even superior, levels.*

It was exciting beyond measure. It was even a little bit frightening. It seemed clear that we had, at the very least, underestimated every child's potential.

This raised a fascinating question. Suppose we looked at three seven-year-old children: Albert, who had half his brain in the jar; Billy, who had a perfectly normal brain; and Charley, who had been treated nonsurgically and who now performed in a totally normal way, although he still had millions of brain cells dead and gone.

Albert, with half his brain gone, was as intelligent as Billy. So was Charley, with millions of dead cells in his head.

What was wrong with nice, average, unhurt Billy?

What was wrong with *well* children?

For years our work had been charged with the vibrancy that one feels prior to important events and great discoveries. Through the years the all-enveloping *fog* of mystery which surrounded our brain-injured children had gradually dispelled. We had also begun to see other facts for which we had not bargained. These were facts about well children. A logical connection had emerged between the brain-injured (and therefore neurologically disorganized) child and the well (and therefore neurologically organized) child, where earlier there were only disconnected and disassociated facts about well children. That logical sequence, as it emerged, had pointed insistently to a path by which we might markedly change man himself—and for the better. Was the neurological organization displayed by an average child necessarily the end of the path?

Now with brain-injured children performing as well as, or better than, average children, the possibility of the path extending farther could be fully seen.

It had always been assumed that neurological growth and its end product, ability, were a static and irrevocable fact: This child was capable and that child was not. This child was bright and that child was not.

Nothing could be further from the truth.

The fact is that neurological growth, which we had always considered a static and irrevocable fact, is a dynamic and ever-changing process. In the severely brain-injured child we see the process of neurological growth totally *halted.*

In the "developmentally delayed" child we see this process of neurological growth considerably *slowed.*

In the average child it takes place at an *average* rate, and in the superior child, at *above-average* speed.

We had now come to realize that the brain-injured child, the average child, and the superior child are not three different kinds of children but instead represent a continuum ranging from the extreme neurological disorganization which severe brain injury creates, through the more moderate neurological disorganization caused by mild or moderate brain injury, through the average amount of neurological organization which the average child demonstrates, to the high degree of neurological organization which a superior child invariably demonstrates.

In the severely brain-injured child we had succeeded in restarting this process which had come to a halt, and in the "developmentally delayed" child we had accelerated it.

It was now clear that this process of neurological growth could be *speeded* as well as delayed. Having repeatedly brought brain-injured children from neurological disorganization to neurological organization of an average or even superior level by employing the simple nonsurgical program that had been developed, there was every reason to believe that this same program could be used to increase the amount of neurological organization demonstrated by average children. Part of this program is to teach very young brain-injured children to read.

Nowhere is the ability to raise neurological organization more clearly demonstrated than when you teach a well baby to read.

a birthday note
for our parents

Dreams don't cost anything.

Forty years ago we dreamed of a world full of children who were intellectually, physically, and socially superb.

We knew that all children have tremendous potential and ability. We were absolutely convinced that tiny kids could learn absolutely anything if we were smart enough to teach it properly.

We imagined that we would not have to wait for a thousand happy accidents to have such children but rather that we could raise our children on purpose.

We believed that if parents knew how the brain grows and why it grows the way that it does that parents would lead the way.

Sometimes our parents traded a second car, a better vacation, or a more comfortable and financially secure life for the privilege of being at home with their own children and teaching them. Our mothers and fathers have always been characterized by the fact that they would rather be with their own children than with anyone else in the world.

Now we can look back over the last forty years and ask how have we done?

What are our children like? Are they as good as we hoped they would be? Where are they headed now? Are they going to change the world for the better? What kind of parents will they be?

Some of the answers to these questions are in this third edition of the book.

Are they as good as we hoped they would be? The answer is no, they are not as good as we hoped they would be.

They are much, much better.

They do many different things and they do all of them well.

As you read their stories in the letters from their mothers and fathers, you may get the impression that these children move through their lives with an ease and confidence that is rare in young people today. Your impression is correct.

Many parents say that the pleasure of being with their children, teaching them to read, and watching them grow each day was the single greatest experience of their lives.

If you give a tiny child lots of love and attention *and* teach him to read, will he be a more loving, more sensitive, more intelligent, and a more capable child than he would have been?

The answer is yes.

Well done to all the mothers and fathers who have taught their babies to read since this book was first published forty years ago. What a magnificent job you have done. Now you have another forty plus years to enjoy the fruits of your loving labor. Don't forget to save those reading cards for your grandchildren.

Well done to each and every child. You have made us proud. Now get on with fixing up this planet—it needs you very, very badly.

Any predictions for the next forty years?

Let the dreaming begin.

1
the facts and Tommy

I've been telling you he can read.

—MR. LUNSKI

It began spontaneously, this gentle revolution.
The strange thing about it is that it came about
in the end by accident.

The kids, who *are* the gentle revolutionaries,
didn't know that they would be able to read if
the tools were given them, and the adults in the
television industry, who finally furnished them,
knew neither that the children had the ability nor
that television would supply the tools which would
bring about the gentle revolution.

The lack of tools is the reason it took so long for it to occur, but now that it's here, we parents must become conspirators in fostering this splendid revolution, not to make it less gentle but to make it more rapid so that the kids can reap its rewards.

It's astonishing really, that the secret has not been discovered by the kids long before this. It's a wonder that they, with all their brightness—because bright they are—didn't catch on.

The only reason some adult hasn't given the secret away to the two-year-olds is that we adults haven't known it either. Of course, if we had known, we would never have allowed it to remain a secret because it's far too important to the kids and to us too.

The trouble is that we have made the print too small.

The trouble is that we have made the print too small.

The trouble is that we have made the print too small.

The trouble is that we have made the print too small.

It is even possible to make the print too small for the sophisticated visual pathway—which includes the brain—of the adult to read.

It is almost impossible to make the print too big to read.

But it *is* possible to make it too small, and that's just what we've done.

The underdeveloped visual pathway, from the eye through the visual areas of the brain itself, of the one-, two-, or three-year-old just can't differentiate one word from another.

But now, as we've said, television has given away the whole secret—through commercials. The result is that when the man on television says, *Gulf, Gulf, Gulf,* in a nice clear, loud voice and the television screen shows the word **GULF** in nice big, clear letters, the kids all learn to recognize the word—and they don't even know the alphabet.

For the truth is that tiny children can learn to read. It is safe to say that in particular very young children can read, *provided* that, in the beginning, you make the print very big.

But we know both of those things now.

Now that we know we have got to do something about it, because what will happen when we teach all the little kids to read will be very important to the world.

But isn't it easier for a child to understand a spoken word rather than a written one? Not at all. The child's brain, which is the only organ that has learning capacity, "hears" the clear, loud television words through the ear and interprets them as only the brain can. Simultaneously the child's brain "sees" the big, clear television words through his eye and interprets them in exactly the same manner. It makes no difference to the brain whether it "sees" a sight or "hears" a sound. It can understand both equally well. All that is required is that the sounds be loud enough and clear enough for the ear to hear and the words big enough and clear enough for the eye to see so that the brain can interpret them—the former we have done but the latter we have failed to do.

People have probably always talked to children in a louder voice than they use with adults, and we still do so, instinctively realizing that children cannot hear and simultaneously understand normal adult conversational tones. Everyone talks loudly to children, and the younger the child is the louder we talk.

Suppose, for the sake of argument, that we adults had long ago decided to speak to each other in sounds just soft enough so that no child could hear and understand them. Suppose, however, that these sounds were just loud enough for his auditory pathway to have become sufficiently sophisticated to hear and understand soft sounds when he got to be six years of age.

Under this set of circumstances we would probably give children "hearing readiness" tests at six years of age. If we found that he could "hear" but not understand words (which would certainly be the case, since his auditory pathway could not distinguish soft sounds until now), it is possible that we would now introduce him to the spoken language by saying the letter A to him, and then B, and so on until he had learned the alphabet, before beginning to teach him how words sound.

One is led to conclude that perhaps there would be a great many children with a problem of "hearing" words and sentences, and that instead of Rudolf Flesch's well-known book called *Why Johnny Can't Read,* we would need a book called *Why Johnny Can't Hear.*

The above is precisely what we have done with written language. We have made it too small for the child to "see and understand" it.

Now let's make another supposition.

If we had spoken in whispers while simultaneously writing words and sentences very large and distinct, very young children would be able to read but would be unable to understand verbal language.

Now suppose that television were introduced with its big written words and with loud spoken words to go with them. Naturally all kids could read the words, but there would also be many children who would begin to understand the spoken word at the astonishing age of two or three.

And that, in reverse, is what is happening today in reading!

TV has also shown us several other interesting

things about children.

The first is that youngsters watch most "kiddie programs" without paying constant attention; but as everyone knows, when the commercials come on the children run to the television set to *hear* about and *read* about what the products contain and what they are supposed to do.

The point here is not that television commercials are pitched to the two-year-old set, nor is it that gasoline or what it contains has any special fascination for two-year-olds, because it does not.

The truth is that the children can *learn* from commercials with the big enough, clear enough, loud enough, repeated message and that all children have a rage to learn.

Children would rather *learn* about something than simply be amused by Mickey Mouse—and that's a fact.

As a result then, the kids ride down the road in the family car and blithely read the Gulf sign, the McDonald's sign and the Coca-Cola sign as well as many others—and *that's* a fact.

There is no need to ask the question, *"Can* very small children learn to read?" They've answered that, they *can*. The question that should be asked is, *"What* do we want children to read?" Should we restrict their reading to the names of products and the rather strange chemicals that these products or our stomachs contain, or should we let them read something which might enrich their lives and which might be a part of Maplewood Avenue rather than Madison Avenue?

Let's look at all of the basic facts:

1. Tiny children *want* to learn to read.
2. Tiny children *can* learn to read.
3. Tiny children *are* learning to read.
4. Tiny children *should* learn to read.

We shall devote a chapter to each of these four facts. Each of them is true and each is simple. Perhaps that has been a large part of the problem. *There are few disguises harder to penetrate than the deceptive cloak of simplicity.*

It was probably this very simplicity that made it difficult for us to understand, or even to believe, the absurd story that Mr. Lunski told us about Tommy.

It's strange that it took us so long to pay any attention to Mr. Lunski, because when we first saw Tommy at The Institutes we were already aware of all the things we needed to know in order to understand what was happening to Tommy.

Tommy was the fourth child in the Lunski family. The Lunski parents hadn't had much time for formal schooling and had worked very hard to support their three nice, normal children. By the time Tommy was born, Mr. Lunski owned a taproom and things were looking up.

However, Tommy was born very severely brain-injured. When he was two years old he was admitted for neurosurgical examination at a fine hospital in New Jersey. The day Tommy was discharged the chief neurosurgeon had a frank talk with Mr. and Mrs. Lunski. The doctor explained that his studies had shown that Tommy was a vegetable-like child who would never walk or talk and should therefore be placed in an institution for life.

All of Mr. Lunski's determined Polish ancestry reinforced his American stubbornness as he stood up to his great height, hitched up his considerable girth and announced, "Doc, you're all mixed up. That's *our* kid."

The Lunskis spent many months searching for someone who would tell them that it didn't necessarily have to be that way. The answers were all the same.

By Tommy's third birthday, however, they had found Dr. Eugene Spitz, chief of neurosurgery at Children's Hospital in Philadelphia.

After carefully making his own neurosurgical studies, Dr. Spitz told the parents that while Tommy was indeed severely brain-injured, perhaps something might be done for him at a group of institutions in a suburb called Chestnut Hill.

Tommy arrived at The Institutes for the Achievement of Human Potential when he was just three years and two weeks old. He could not move or talk.

Tommy's brain injury and his resultant problems were evaluated at The Institutes. A treatment program was prescribed for Tommy which would reproduce the normal developmental growth of well children in Tommy. The parents were taught how to carry out this program at home and were told that if they adhered to it without failure, Tommy might be greatly improved. They were to return in sixty days for a re-evaluation, and if Tommy were improved, for program revisions.

There was no question but that the Lunskis would follow the strict program. They did so with religious intensity.

By the time they returned for the second visit, Tommy could creep.

Now the Lunskis attacked the program with energy inspired by success. So determined were they that when their car broke down on the way to Philadelphia for the third visit, they simply bought a used car and continued to their appointment. They could hardly wait to tell us that Tommy could now say his first two words— "Mommy" and "Daddy." Tommy was now three and a half and could creep on hands and knees.

Then his mother tried something only a mother would try with a child like Tommy. In much the same manner that a father buys a football for his infant son, Mother bought an alphabet book for her three-and-a-half-year-old, severely brain-injured, two-word-speaking son. Tommy, she announced, was very bright, whether he could walk and talk or not. Anyone who had any sense could see it simply by looking in his eyes!

While our tests for intelligence in brain-injured children during those days were a good deal more involved than Mrs. Lunski's, they were no more accurate than hers. We agreed that Tommy was intelligent all right, but to teach a brain-injured three-and-a-half-year-old to read—well, that was another question.

We paid very little attention when Mrs. Lunski announced that Tommy, then four years of age, could read *all* of the *words* in the alphabet book even more easily than he could read the letters. We were more concerned and pleased with his speech, which was progressing constantly, as was his physical mobility.

By the time Tommy was four years and two months old his father announced that he could read all of a Dr. Seuss book called *Green Eggs and Ham*. We smiled politely and noted how remarkably Tommy's speech and movement were improving.

When Tommy was four years and six months old Mr. Lunski announced that Tommy could read, and had read, *all* of the Dr. Seuss books. We noted on the chart that Tommy was progressing beautifully, as well as the fact that Mr. Lunski "said" Tommy could read.

When Tommy arrived for his eleventh visit he had just had his fifth birthday. Although both Dr. Spitz and we were delighted with the superb advances Tommy was making, there was nothing to indicate at the beginning of the visit that this day would be an important one for all children. Nothing, that is, except Mr. Lunski's usual nonsensical report. Tommy, Mr. Lunski announced, could now read anything, including the *Reader's Digest,* and what was more, he could understand it, and what was more than that, he'd started doing it before his fifth birthday.

We were saved from the necessity of having to comment on this by the arrival of one of the kitchen staff with our lunch—tomato juice and a hamburger. Mr. Lunski, noting our lack of response, took a piece of paper from the desk and wrote, "Glenn Doman likes to drink tomato juice and eat hamburger."

Tommy, following his father's instructions, read this easily and with the proper accents and inflections. He did not hesitate as does the seven-year-old, reading each word separately without understanding of the sentence itself.

"Write another sentence," we said slowly.

Mr. Lunski wrote, "Tommy's daddy likes to drink beer and whiskey. He has a great big fat belly from drinking beer and whiskey at Tommy's Tavern."

Tommy had read only the first three words aloud when he began to laugh. The funny part about Dad's belly was down on the fourth line since Mr. Lunski was writing in large letters.

This severely brain-injured little child was actually reading much faster than he was reciting the words aloud at his normal speaking rate. Tommy was not only reading, he was speed-reading and his comprehension was obvious!

The fact that we were thunderstruck was written on our faces. We turned to Mr. Lunski.

"I've been telling you he can read," said Mr. Lunski.

After that day none of us would ever be the same, for this was the last piece of puzzle in a pattern which had been forming for more than twenty years.

Tommy had taught us that even a severely brain-injured child can learn to read far earlier than normal children usually do.

Tommy, of course, was immediately subjected to full-scale testing by a group of experts who were brought from Washington, D.C., for this purpose within a week. Tommy—severely brain-injured and just barely five years old—could read better than the average child twice his age—and with complete comprehension.

By the time Tommy was six he walked, although this was relatively new to him and he was still a little shaky; he read at the sixth-grade level (eleven- to twelve-year-old level). Tommy was not going to spend his life in an institution, but his parents were looking for a "special" school to put Tommy in come the following September. Special *high,* that is, not special low. Fortunately there are schools now for exceptional "gifted" children. Tommy has had the dubious "gift" of severe brain injury and the unquestionable gift of parents who love him very much indeed and who believed that at least one kid wasn't achieving his potential.

Tommy, in the end, was a catalyst for twenty years of study. Maybe it would be more accurate to say he was a fuse for an explosive charge that had been growing in force for twenty years.

The fascinating thing was that Tommy *wanted* very much to read and enjoyed it tremendously.

2
tiny children
want to learn
to read

*It has me beaten, we haven't been able to
stop her reading since she was three.*

—MRS. GILCHRIST,
MOTHER OF FOUR-YEAR-OLD MARY,
Newsweek

There has never been, in the history of man, an
adult scientist who has been half so curious as is
any child between the ages of eighteen months and
four years. We adults have mistaken this superb
curiosity about everything as a lack of ability to
concentrate.

We have, of course, observed our children carefully, but we have not always understood what
their actions mean. For one thing, many people

often use two very different words as if they were the same. The words are *learn* and *educate*.

The *American College Dictionary* tells us that *learn* means: "1. To acquire knowledge of or skill in by study, instruction, or experience..."

To *educate* means: "1. To develop the faculties and powers of by teaching, instruction, or schooling...and 2. To provide education for; send to school..."

In other words, learning generally refers to the process that goes on in the one who is acquiring knowledge, while educating is often the learning process guided by a teacher or school. Although everyone really knows this, these two processes are frequently thought of as one and the same.

Because of this we sometimes feel that since formal *education* begins at six years of age, the more important processes of learning also begin at six years of age.

Nothing could be further from the truth.

The truth is that a child begins to learn just after birth. By the time he is six years of age and begins his schooling he has already absorbed a fantastic amount of information, fact for fact, perhaps more than he will learn the rest of his life.

By the time a child is six he has learned most of the basic facts about himself and his family. He has learned about his neighbors and his relationships to them, his world and his relationship to it, and a host of other facts which are literally uncountable. Most significantly, he has learned at least one whole language and sometimes more than one. (The chances are very small that he will ever truly master an additional language after he is six.)

All this before he has seen the inside of a classroom.

The process of learning through these years proceeds at great speed unless we thwart it. If we appreciate and encourage it, the process will take place at a truly unbelievable rate.

A tiny child has, burning within him, a boundless desire to learn.

We can kill this desire entirely only by destroying him completely.

We can come close to quenching it by isolating him. We read occasionally of, say, a thirteen-year-old idiot who is found in an attic chained to a bedpost, presumably because he was an idiot. The reverse is probably the case. It is extremely likely that he is an idiot because he was chained to the bedpost. To appreciate this fact we must realize that only psychotic parents would chain any child. A parent chains a child to a bedpost *because* the parent is psychotic, and the result is a profoundly hurt child *because* he has been denied virtually all opportunity to learn.

We can *diminish* the child's desire to *learn* by

limiting the experiences to which we expose him. Unhappily we have done this almost universally by drastically underestimating what he can learn.

We can *increase* his learning markedly, simply by removing many of the physical restrictions we have placed upon him.

We can *multiply* by many times the knowledge he absorbs and even his potential if we appreciate his superb capacity for learning and give him unlimited opportunity while simultaneously encouraging him to do so.

Throughout history there have been isolated but numerous cases of people who have actually taught tiny children to read, and do other advanced things, by appreciating and encouraging them. In *all* of the cases which we were able to find, the results of such preplanned home opportunity for children to learn ranged from "excellent" to "astonishing" in producing happy, well-adjusted children with exceptionally high intelligence.

It is very important to bear in mind that these children had *not* been found to have high intelligence first and then been given unusual opportunities to learn, but instead were simply children whose parents decided to expose them to as much information as possible at a very early age.

Throughout history the great teachers have pointed out again and again that we must foster a love of learning in our children. Unhappily they have not told us often enough how we might do this. The ancient Hebrew scholars taught parents to bake cakes in the form of the letters of the Hebrew alphabet which the child had to identify before he was allowed to eat the cake. In a similar way, Hebrew words were written with honey on the child's slate. The child would then read the words and lick them off so that "the words of the law might be sweet on his lips."

Once an adult who cares about children is made sensitive to what a young child is really doing, he wonders how he could ever have missed it in the first place.

Look carefully at the eighteen-month-old child and see what he does.

In the first place he drives everybody to distraction.

Why does he? Because he won't stop being curious. He cannot be dissuaded, disciplined, or confined out of this desire to learn, no matter how hard we try—and we have certainly tried very hard.

He wants to learn about the lamp and the coffee cup and the electric light socket and the newspaper and everything else in the room—which means that he knocks over the lamp, spills the coffee cup, puts his finger in the electric light socket, and tears up the newspaper. He is learning constantly and, quite naturally, we can't stand it.

From the way he carries on we have concluded that he is hyperactive and unable to pay attention, when the simple truth is that he pays attention to everything. He is superbly alert in every way he can be to learn about the world. He sees, hears, feels, smells, and tastes. There is no other way to learn except by these five routes into the brain, and the child uses them all.

He sees the lamp and therefore pulls it down so that he can feel it, hear it, look at it, smell it, and taste it. Given the opportunity, he will do all these things to the lamp—and he will do the same to every object in the room. He will not demand to be let out of the room until he has absorbed all he can, through every sense available to him, about every object in the room. He is doing his best to learn and, of course, we are doing our best to stop him because his learning process is far too expensive.

We parents have devised several methods of coping with the curiosity of the very young child and, unfortunately, almost all of them are at the expense of the child's learning.

The first general method is the give-him-something-to-play-with-that-he-can't-break school of thought. This usually means a nice pink rattle to play with. It may even be a more complicated toy than a rattle, but it's still a toy. Presented with such an object the child promptly looks at it (which is why toys have bright colors), bangs it to find out if it makes a noise (which is why rattles rattle), feels it (which is why toys don't have sharp edges), tastes it (which is why the paint is non-poisonous), and even smells it (we have not yet figured out how toys ought to smell, which is why they don't smell at all). This process takes about ninety seconds.

Now that he knows all he wants to know about the toy for the present, the child promptly abandons it and turns his attention to the box in which it came. The child finds the box just as interesting as the toy—which is why we should always buy toys that come in boxes—and learns all about the box. This also takes about ninety seconds. In fact, the child will frequently pay more attention to the box than to the toy itself. Because he is allowed to break the box, he may be able to learn how it is made. This is an advantage he does not have with the toy itself since we make toys unbreakable, which of course reduces his ability to learn.

Therefore it would seem that buying a child a toy that comes in a box would be a good way to double his attention span. But have we—or have we merely given him twice as much interesting material? It is quite clear that the latter is the case. In short, we must conclude that a child's attention span is related to the amount of material he has available to learn about rather than believing, as we often do, that a child is incapable of paying attention for very long.

If you simply watch children, you will see dozens of examples of this. Yet, despite all of the evidence that our eyes give us, we too often come to the conclusion that when a child has a short attention span, he just isn't very smart. This deduction insidiously implies that he (like all other children) is not very bright because he is very young. One wonders what our conclusions would be if the two-year-old sat in a corner and quietly played with the rattle for five hours. Probably the parents of such a child would be even more upset—and with good reason.

The second general method of coping with his attempts to learn is the put-him-back-in-the-playpen school of thought.

The only proper thing about the playpen is its name—it is truly a pen. We should at least be honest about such devices and stop saying, "Let's go buy a playpen for the baby." Let's tell the truth and admit that we buy them for ourselves.

There is a cartoon which shows Mother sitting in a playpen, reading and smiling contentedly while the children play outside the pen, unable to get at her. This cartoon, aside from its humorous element, also suggests another truth: The mother who already knows about the world can afford to be isolated, while the children outside, who have much to learn, can continue their explorations.

Few parents realize what a playpen really costs. Not only does the playpen restrict the child's ability to learn about the world, which is fairly obvious, but it seriously restricts his neurological growth by limiting his ability to crawl and creep (processes vital to normal growth). This in turn inhibits the development of his vision, manual competence, hand-eye coordination, and a host of other things.

We parents have persuaded ourselves that we are buying the playpen to protect the child from hurting himself by chewing on an electric cord or falling down the stairs. Actually we are penning him up so that *we* do not have to make sure he is safe. In terms of our time we are being penny-wise and pound-foolish.

How much more sensible it would be, if we must have a playpen, to use one which is twelve feet long and twenty-four inches wide so that the baby may crawl, creep, and learn during these vital years of his life. With such a playpen the child can move twelve feet by crawling or creeping in a straight line before he finds himself against the side at the opposite end. Such a playpen is infinitely more convenient to parents also, since it only takes up space along one wall rather than filling up the room.

The playpen as an implement to prevent learning is unfortunately much more effective than the rattle, because after the child has spent ninety seconds learning about each toy Mother puts in (which is why he will throw each of them out as he finishes learning about it), he is then stuck.

Thus we have succeeded in preventing him from destroying things (one way of learning) by physically confining him. This approach, which puts the child in a physical, emotional, and educational vacuum, will not fail so long as we can stand his anguished screams to get out; or, assuming that we can stand it, until he's big enough to climb out and renew his search for learning.

Does all the above assume that we are in favor of the child breaking the lamp? Not at all. It assumes only that we have had far too little respect for the small child's desire to learn, despite all the clear indications he gives us *that he wants desperately to learn everything he can, and as quickly as possible.*

Apocryphal stories keep creeping up which, even if they are not true, are revealing nevertheless.

There is the story of the two five-year-old kindergarten boys standing in the schoolyard when a plane flashes by overhead. One youngster says that the airplane is supersonic. The other refutes this on the basis that the wings are not swept back enough. The recess bell interrupts the discussion and the first child says, "We've got to stop now and go back to stringing those damned beads."

The story is overdrawn, but true in implication.

Consider the three-year-old who asks, "Daddy, why is the sun hot?" "How did the little man get into the TV set?" "What makes the flowers grow, Mommy?"

While the child is displaying an electronic, astronomical, and biological curiosity, we too often tell him to run along and play with his toys. Simultaneously we may well be concluding that because he is very young he wouldn't understand and, besides, that he has a very short attention span. He certainly has—for most toys, at least.

We have succeeded in keeping our children carefully isolated from learning in a period of life when the desire to learn is at its peak.

The human brain is unique in that it is the only container of which it can be said that the more you put into it, the more it will hold.

Between nine months and four years the ability to absorb information is unparalleled, and the desire to do so is higher than it will ever be again. Yet during this period we keep the child clean, well fed, safe from the world about him—and in a learning vacuum.

It is ironic that when the child is older we will

tell him repeatedly how foolish he is for not wanting to learn about astronomy, physics, and biology. Learning, we will tell him, is the most important thing in life, and indeed it is.

We have, however, overlooked the other side of the coin.

Learning is also the greatest game in life, and the most fun.

We have assumed that children hate to learn essentially because most of us have disliked or even despised school. Again we have mistaken schooling for learning. Not all children in school are learning—just as not all children who are learning are doing so in school.

My own experiences in first grade were perhaps typical of what they have been for centuries. In general the teacher told us to sit down, keep quiet, look at her, and listen to her while she began a process called teaching which, she said, would be mutually painful but from which we would learn—or else.

In my own case, that first-grade teacher's prophecy proved to be correct; it was painful and, at least for the first twelve years, I hated every minute of it. I'm sure it was not a unique experience.

The process of learning should be fun of the highest order, for it is indeed the greatest game in life. Sooner or later all bright people come to this conclusion. Time and again you hear people say, "It was a great day. I learned a great many things I didn't know before." One even hears, "I had a terrible day *but* I learned something."

A recent experience, which climaxed hundreds of similar but less amusing situations, serves as an excellent example of the fact that tiny children want to learn to the degree that they are unable to distinguish learning from fun. They keep this attitude until we adults convince them that learning is *not* fun.

Our team had been seeing a brain-injured three-year-old child for a number of months and she had reached the point where it was time to introduce her to reading. It was important to this child's rehabilitation that she learn to read, because it is impossible to inhibit a single human brain function without to some degree suppressing the total sum of brain function. Conversely, if we teach a very young brain-injured child to read we will assist materially in his speech and other functions. It was for this reason that we had prescribed that this child be taught to read upon this particular visit.

The child's father was, understandably, skeptical about teaching his brain-injured three-year-old daughter to read. He was persuaded to do so only because of the splendid physical and speech progress that the child had made up to this time.

When he returned for a progress check two months later, he gleefully told the following story: While he had agreed to do as he had been instructed, he did not believe that it would work. He had also decided that if he was going to try to teach his brain-injured child to read, he was going to do it in what he considered to be a "typical classroom environment."

He had, therefore, built a schoolroom, complete with blackboard and desks, in his basement. He had then invited his well seven-year-old daughter to attend also.

Predictably, the seven-year-old had taken one look at the classroom and yelped with joy. She had the biggest toy in the whole neighborhood. Bigger than a baby carriage, bigger than a doll house. She had her own private school.

In July the seven-year-old went out into the neighborhood and recruited five children, ranging from three to five years of age, to "play school."

Of course they were excited by the idea and agreed to be good children so they could go to school like their older brothers and sisters. They played school five days a week all summer long. The seven-year-old was the teacher and the smaller children were her pupils.

The children were not forced to play this game. It was simply the best game they had ever found to play.

The "school" closed down in September when the seven-year-old teacher went back to her own second grade.

As a result, in that particular neighborhood there are now five children, ranging in age from three to five years, who can read. They can't read Shakespeare, but they can read the twenty-five words that the seven-year-old teacher taught them. They read them and they understand them.

Surely this seven-year-old must be listed among the most accomplished educators in history—or else we must conclude that three-year-olds *want* to read.

We choose to believe that it is the three-year-old's desire to read rather than the seven-year-old's teaching skill which makes for learning.

Finally it is important to note that when a three-year-old is taught to read a book, he can pay attention to the book for long periods of time, appears to be very bright, and stops smashing lamps altogether; but he is still only three years old and still finds most toys to be of interest for about ninety seconds.

While, naturally, no child wants specifically to learn to read until he knows that reading exists, all children want to absorb information about everything around them, and under the proper circumstances reading is one of these things.

3
tiny children
can learn
to read

One day not long ago I found her on the living-room floor thumbing through a French book. She simply told me, "Well, Mummy, I've read all the English books in the house."

—MRS. GILCHRIST,
Newsweek

Very young children can and do learn to read words, sentences, and paragraphs in exactly the same way they learn to understand spoken words, sentences, and paragraphs.

Again the facts are simple—beautiful but simple. We have already stated that the eye sees but does not understand what is seen and that the ear hears but does not understand what is heard. Only the brain understands.

When the ear apprehends, or picks up, a spoken word or message, this auditory message is broken down into a series of electrochemical impulses and flashed to the unhearing brain, which then reassembles and *comprehends* in terms of the meaning the word was intended to convey.

In precisely the same manner it happens that when the eye apprehends a printed word or message, this visual message is broken down into a series of electrochemical impulses and flashed to the unseeing brain to be reassembled and comprehended as reading.

It is a magical instrument, the brain.

Both the visual pathway and the auditory pathway travel through the brain where *both* messages are interpreted by the same brain process.

Visual *acuity* and auditory *acuity* actually have very little to do with it, unless they are very poor indeed.

There are many animals that see or hear better than any human being. Nonetheless, no chimpanzee, no matter how acute his vision or hearing, has yet read the word "freedom" through his eye or understood it through his ear. He hasn't the brain for it.

To begin understanding the human brain we must consider the instant of conception rather than the moment of birth, because the superb and very little understood process of brain growth begins at conception.

From conception on, the human brain grows at an explosive rate which is continually on a descending scale.

Explosive and *descending.*

The whole process is essentially complete at the age of six.

At conception the fertile egg is microscopic in size. Twelve days later the embryo is large enough so that the brain can be differentiated. This is long before Mother knows she is pregnant, so phenomenally fast is the rate of growth.

While the *rate* of growth is fantastic, this rate is always slower than the day before.

By birth the child weighs six or seven pounds, which is millions of times what the egg weighed nine months earlier at conception. It is obvious that if his *rate* of growth were the same in the next nine months as it was in the previous nine months, he would weigh thousands of tons when he was nine months old and many millions of tons when he was eighteen months old.

The process of brain growth matches the body growth but is on an even more descending rate. This can be seen clearly when one appreciates the fact that at birth the child's brain makes up 11 percent of the total body weight, while in adults it's only 2.5 percent.

When the child is five the growth of the brain is 80 percent complete.

When he is six the process of brain growth is, as we have said, virtually complete.

During the years between six and sixty we have less brain growth than we had in the single year (and slowest of the first six years) between the ages of five and six.

In addition to this basic understanding of how the brain grows, it is important to understand which of its functions are most important to humans.

There are just six neurological functions which are exclusive to man, and these six functions characterize man and set him apart from other creatures.

These are the six functions of a layer of the brain known as the *human* cortex. These exclusively human abilities are present and functioning by six years of age. They are worth knowing.

1. Only man is able to walk entirely upright.
2. Only man speaks in abstract, symbolic, devised language.
3. Only man is able to combine his unique manual competence with motor abilities listed above to write his language.

The first three skills listed are of a *motor* nature (expressive) and are based upon the remaining three, which are *sensory* in nature (receptive).

4. Only man understands the abstract, symbolic, devised language which he hears.

5. Only man sees in a manner which enables him to read the abstract language when it is in written form.

6. Only man can identify an object by touch alone.

A six-year-old child is capable of all of these functions since he walks, talks, writes, reads, understands spoken language, and identifies objects by touch at that age. It is evident that from that time on we are simply talking about a sort of lateral multiplication of these six exclusively human abilities, rather than the addition of new ones.

Since all of man's later life is, to a large degree, dependent upon these six functions, which are developed in the first six years of life, an investigation and description of the various phases which exist during that molding period of life is very important.

THE PERIOD FROM BIRTH TO ONE

This period of life is *vital* to the child's whole future.

It is true that we keep him warm, fed, and clean, but we also seriously restrict his neurological growth.

What *should* happen to him during this time could easily be the subject of a whole book. Suffice it to say here that during this period of life the infant should have almost unlimited opportunity for movement, for physical exploration, and for experience. Our present society and culture usually deny him this. Such opportunity, on the rare occasions when it is afforded a child, results in physically and neurologically superior children. *What the adult will be in terms of physical and neurological ability is determined more strongly in this period than in any other.*

THE PERIOD FROM ONE TO FIVE

This period of life is *crucial* to the child's whole future.

During this period of life we love him, make sure he doesn't hurt himself, smother him with toys, and send him to nursery school. And, totally unaware, we are doing our best to prevent learning.

What *should* happen to him during these crucial years is that we should be satisfying his staggering thirst for raw material, which he wants to soak up in all possible forms but particularly in terms of language, whether spoken and heard or printed and read.

It is during this period of life that the child should learn to read, thus unlocking the door to the golden treasury of all things written by man in history, the sum of man's knowledge. It is during these not-to-be-relived years, these years of insatiable curiosity, that the child's whole intellectual being will be established. What the child can be, what his interests will be, what his capacities will be, are being determined in these years. An unlimited number of factors will bear on him as an adult. Friends, society, and culture may influence what job he will do in life, and some of these factors may be harmful to his full potential.

While such circumstances of adult life may combine to lower his capacity to enjoy life and to be productive, he will not rise above the potential that is established during this crucial period of his life. It is for this all-important reason that every opportunity should be given the child to gain knowledge, which he enjoys beyond all other things.

It is ridiculous to assume that when a child's insatiable curiosity is being satisfied, and in a manner which he adores, we are depriving him of his precious childhood. Such an attitude would be completely unworthy of mention, were it not so frequently encountered. One rarely finds parents, however, who believe that there is any loss of "precious childhood" when they see the eagerness with which a child engages himself in reading a book with Mommy, as compared to his anguished screams to get out of the playpen or his total boredom in the midst of a mountain of toys.

Learning during this period of life is, moreover, a compelling necessity and we are thwarting all of nature when we try to prevent it. *It is necessary for survival.*

The kitten that "plays" by leaping upon the ball of wool is simply using the wool as a substitute for a mouse. The puppy that "plays" in mock ferocity with other puppies is learning how to survive when attacked.

Survival in the human world is dependent upon the ability to communicate, and language is the tool of communication.

The child's play, like the kitten's play, is purposeful and aimed at learning rather than amusement.

The acquisition of language in all of its forms is one of the prime purposes for the child's play. We must be careful to see it for what it is rather than assume that such play is geared toward amusement.

The need to learn during this period of life is, for the child, a stark necessity. Isn't it wonderful that an omniscient Nature made the child also love learning? Isn't it awful that we have so terribly misunderstood what a child is, and placed so many roadblocks in Nature's way? This then is the period of life in which the child's brain is an open door to all information. During this period of life he takes in all information without conscious effort of any sort. This is the period of life in which he can learn to read easily and naturally. He should be given the opportunity to do so.

It is during this period that he can learn to speak a foreign language, even as many as five, which he at present fails to learn through high school and college. They should be offered to him. He will learn easily now, but with great difficulty later.

It is during this period that he should be exposed to all the basic information about written language, which he now learns with much effort between the ages of six and ten. He will learn it more quickly and easily.

It is more than a unique opportunity, it is a sacred duty. We must open the floodgate of all basic knowledge to him.

We shall never again have an equal opportunity.

THE PERIOD FROM FIVE TO SIX

This period of life is *very important* to the child's whole life.

During this important time, which is virtually the end of his plastic, pliable, formative days, he begins school. What a traumatic period of life this can be! What reader does not remember this part of his life, no matter how long ago it may have been? The experience of entering kindergarten and the year that follows is frequently the earliest memory that an adult retains. Often it is not remembered with pleasure.

Why should this be, when children want so desperately to learn? Can we interpret this to mean that a child does not want to learn? Or is it more likely that this indicates we are making a very basic and important mistake?

If we are making such a basic mistake, what could it be? Consider the facts in the case.

In some cases, we are suddenly taking this child who, up until now, has probably spent little, if any, time away from home, and introducing him to an entirely new physical and social world. It would be an indictment of his happiness in the home situation if the five- or six-year-old did not miss home and Mother during this very important formative period of life. Simultaneously we begin to introduce him to group discipline and early education.

We must remember that the child is long on the ability to learn but still very short on judgment. The result is that the child associates the unhappiness of being suddenly away from Mother with the early educational experience, and thus from the beginning the child associates learning with what is, at best, a vague unhappiness. This is hardly a fine beginning for the most important job in life.

By doing this we have also dealt the teacher a severe blow. It is little wonder that many teachers face their task with grim determination rather than with joyous anticipation. She has two strikes against her when first she lays eyes on her new pupil.

How much better it would be for pupil, teacher, and the world if, by that first day of school, the new pupil had already acquired and kept a love of the joy of learning.

If this were the case, the child's love of reading and learning, which was now about to be increased, would go a very long way toward minimizing the psychological blow of having Mommy's apron strings cut.

In fact, when a child is introduced to learning at a very young age, it is gratifying to watch the child's love of learning very often become a love of school as well. It is significant that when these children do not feel well, they frequently attempt to conceal it from Mother (usually without success) so that they will not be kept home from school. What a delightful switch on our own childhood experiences when we frequently pretended illness (usually without success) in order *not* to have to go to school.

Our lack of recognition of these basic factors has led us to some very bad psychological actions. From an educational standpoint the seven-year old is beginning to learn to read—but to read about trivia far below his interest, knowledge, and ability.

What *should* be happening to the child during this important period of life between five and six (assuming that the proper things had happened to him in the previous periods) is that he should be enjoying the material which would normally be presented to him when he is between six and fourteen years of age.

That the results of this on a broad scale can only be good is evident, unless we are willing to accept the premise that ignorance leads to good and knowledge to evil; and that playing with a toy must result in happiness, while learning about language and the world means unhappiness.

It would be as silly to assume that filling the brain with information would somehow use it up, while keeping it empty would preserve it.

A person whose brain is loaded with useful information that he can use easily could be rated a genius, while a person whose brain is empty of information is called an idiot.

When this *gentle revolution* in learning began, we could only dream of what effect it would have on children given this new opportunity. However, in 1994 the book *Kids Who Start Ahead, Stay Ahead* by Neil Harvey, Ph.D., reported on what happened intellectually, physically, and socially to 314 early learners when they reached school. During preschool years (0-4) they had been introduced to reading, math, physical activities, the social graces, and a wide variety of general knowledge. Entering school, nearly thirty-five percent of them were classified "gifted." They and the other early learners excelled convincingly in all areas.

The amount of knowledge we have prevented our children from gaining measures our lack of appreciation for his genius to learn. How much they have succeeded in learning *despite* our prevention is a tribute to that same genius for absorbing information.

The newborn child is almost an exact duplicate of an empty electronic computer, although superior to such a computer in almost every way.

An empty computer is capable of receiving a vast amount of information readily and without effort.

So is a tiny child.

A computer is able to classify and file such information.

So is a child.

A computer is able to place such information in either permanent or temporary storage.

So is a child.

You can't expect a computer to give you accurate answers until you have put in the basic information upon which the question you ask is based. The computer cannot.

Neither can a child.

When you have placed sufficient basic information in the computer you will receive correct answers and even judgments from the machine.

So can you from a child.

The machine will accept all information you place in it, whether such information is correct or not.

So will a child.

The machine will reject no information which is entered in the proper form.

Neither will a child.

If incorrect information is put into the machine, future answers based upon this material will be incorrect.

So will the child's.

Here the parallel ends.

If incorrect information is placed in the computer, the machine can be emptied and reprogrammed.

This is not true of a child. The basic information placed in the child's brain for permanent storage has two limitations. The first limitation is that if you put misinformation into his brain during the first six years of life, it is extremely difficult to erase it. The second limitation is that after he is six years of age, he will absorb new material slowly and with greater difficulty.

Consider the Brooklyn child who says "pernt" for "point," the Georgia child who says "heah" for "here," or the Massachusetts child who says "idear" for "idea." Very rarely does travel or education eliminate the local mispronunciation, which is in fact what all accents are, charming as they may sound. Even if later education places a sophisticated veneer over the basic learning of the first six years, a period of great stress will wash it away.

The story is told of a beautiful but uneducated showgirl who married a wealthy man. He went to great lengths to educate his new wife and apparently was successful. But some years later while descending from a carriage in a manner befitting the cultured lady she had become, a priceless string of pearls became entangled in the carriage and broke, scattering the perfect pearls in all directions.

"Bejeesus," she is reported to have shouted, "me beads!"

What is placed in the child's brain during the first six years of life is probably there to stay. We should, therefore, make every effort to make certain it is good and correct. It has been said, "Give me a child for the first six years of life and you can do with him what you will thereafter."

Nothing could be more true.

Everyone knows the ease with which small children memorize material, even material which they don't really understand.

Recently we saw a six-year-old reading in a kitchen in which a dog was barking, a radio was playing, and in which a family argument was reaching a crescendo. The child was memorizing a poem of some length, to be recited in school the next day. He succeeded.

If an adult were asked to learn a poem today to recite before a group tomorrow, chances are that he would be panic-stricken. Supposing that he succeeded in doing so and that six months later he were asked to recite it again. The odds are great that he would be unable to do so, but that he would still remember poems he had recited as a child.

While a child is able to absorb and retain virtually all material presented to him during these vastly important years, his ability to learn the language is unique, and it matters little if this language is spoken, which he learns in an auditory way, or written, which he learns in a visual way.

As has been pointed out, with every passing day the child's ability to take in information without effort *descends*, but it is also true that with each passing day his ability to make judgment goes up. Eventually that downward curve and the upward curve cross each other.

Prior to the time when the curves meet, the child is in some ways actually *superior* to the adult. The ability to learn languages is one of them.

Let's consider this unique factor of superiority in language acquisition.

I spent four years trying to learn French as an adolescent and young adult and have twice been in France, but it is perfectly safe to say that I speak virtually no French. Yet every normal French child learns to speak French well, using all the basic rules of grammar, before he is six years old.

It's sort of upsetting when you think about it.

At first glance one might suspect that the difference is not in the child versus the adult, but instead in the fact that the child was in France while the adult was not, and thus exposed to hearing French all of the time and from every side.

Let's see if that is really the difference or whether the difference lies in the child's unlimited capacity and the adult's great difficulty to learn languages.

Literally tens of thousands of American Army officers have been assigned to foreign countries and many have tried to pick up the new language. Let's take the example of Major John Smith. Major Smith is thirty years of age and a fine physical specimen. He is also a college graduate and has an I.Q. at least fifteen points above average. Major Smith is assigned to a post in Germany.

Major Smith is sent to a German-language school, which he attends three nights a week. The Army language schools are fine institutions for adults, teaching by a system of spoken language and employing the best teachers available.

Major Smith works very hard to learn German, since it is important to his career and since he deals with German-speaking people as well as English-speaking people all day long.

Be all that as it may, a year later when he goes shopping with his five-year-old son, the child does most of the talking for the simple reason that he speaks fairly good German and Major Smith does not.

How can this be?

Dad has been taught German by the best German teacher that the Army can find, and yet, he does not really speak German, while his five-year-old child does!

Who taught the child? Nobody, really. It is just that he was at home during the day with the German-speaking maid. Who taught the maid German? Nobody, really.

Dad was taught German and doesn't speak it.

The child was not taught German and does speak it.

Lest the reader be sucked into the trap of still believing that the difference lies in the slightly different environments of Major Smith and his son rather than in the child's unique ability and the adult's relative inability to learn languages, let us quickly consider the case of *Mrs.* Smith who has lived in the same house with the same maid as the child. Mrs. Smith has learned no more German than has Major Smith and far, far less than her son.

If our misuse of this unique ability to learn languages in childhood were not so sad and wasteful, it would be downright amusing.

If the Smiths happen to have a number of children when they go to Germany, the language proficiency will be directly inverse to the age of the family member.

The three-year-old, if there is one, will learn the most German.

The five-year-old will learn a great deal, but not as much as the three-year-old.

The ten-year-old will learn much German, but less than the five-year-old.

The fifteen-year-old will learn some German, which he will soon forget.

Poor Major and Mrs. Smith will actually learn almost no German at all.

The example which has been given, far from being an isolated case, is almost universally true. We have known children who have learned French or Spanish or German or Japanese or Iranian under these precise circumstances.

Another point we should like to make is not so much the child's innate ability to learn languages as it is the adult's *inability* to learn foreign tongues.

One is horrified when one considers the many millions of dollars that are wasted annually in high schools and colleges in the United States in trying vainly to teach languages to young adults who are almost incapable of learning them.

Let the reader consider if he or she *really* learned a foreign language in high school or in college.

If after four years of school-French the reader was able to struggle through asking a waiter in France for a glass of water, let him try to explain that he wants a glass of *iced* water. This is enough to convince all but the most hardy that four years of French wasn't enough. It's more than enough for any small child.

There is simply no question of the fact that a child, far from being an inferior, small-size adult, is in fact in many ways superior to grownups and that not the least of these ways is his almost uncanny faculty to absorb languages.

We have accepted almost without thought this truly miraculous ability.

Every normal child learns virtually an entire language between the age of one and five.

He learns it with the exact accent of his nation, his state, his city, his neighborhood, and his family. He learns it without visible effort and precisely as it is spoken. Who ever does this again?

Nor does it stop there.

Every child who is raised in a bilingual household will learn *two* languages before he is six years old. Moreover, he will learn the foreign language with the exact accent of the locale in which the parents learned it.

If an American child with Italian parents talks to a true Italian in later life, the Italian will say, "Ah, you are from Milan"—if that's where the parents were reared—"I can tell by your accent." This despite the fact that the Italian-American has never been outside the United States.

Every child who is raised in a trilingual household will speak three foreign languages before he is six years old, and so on.

Years ago, while in Brazil, we met a nine-year-old boy of average intelligence who could understand, read, and write nine languages rather fluently. Avi Roxannes was born in Cairo (French, Arabic, and English) and his (Turkish) grandfather lived with them. When he was four the family moved to Israel where Avi's (Spanish) grandmother on his father's side joined them. In Israel he learned three more languages (Hebrew, German, and Yiddish) and then at six years of age he moved to Brazil (Portuguese).

Since between them the parents speak as many languages as Avi does (but not individually), the Roxannes wisely carry on conversations with him in each of his nine tongues (individually where only one parent speaks a particular language, and collectively where they both do). Avi's parents are a good deal better linguists than most adults, having learned five languages each as children, but of course they are no match at all for Avi when it comes to English or Portuguese, which they learned as adults.

We have previously noted that there have been, in history, many carefully documented cases of what happened when parents have decided to teach very young children to do things which were—and still are—considered extraordinary.

One of these is the case of little Winifred, whose mother, Winifred Sackville Stoner, wrote a book about Winifred called *Natural Education*, which was published in 1914.

This mother began to encourage her child and to give her special opportunities to learn right after birth. We shall discuss the results of this attitude on Winifred's reading later in this book. For now let's see what Mrs. Stoner had to say about her baby's ability with spoken language at five years of age:

"As soon as Winifred could make all her wants known I began to teach her Spanish through conversation and the same direct methods I had used in teaching English. I chose Spanish as her secondary tongue because it is the simplest of European languages. By the time that Winifred reached her fifth milestone she was able to express her thoughts in eight languages, and I have no doubt she could have doubled the number by this time if I had continued our game of word construction in various languages. But at this time I began to think that Esperanto would soon become the international medium of communication, and outside of developing linguistic ability a knowledge of many, many tongues could be of no great benefit to my little girl."

Later Mrs. Stoner says, "The usual methods of teaching languages in school through grammatical rules and transactions have proved an utter failure as regards the ability of pupils to use language as tools for thought expression.

"There are Latin professors who have taught Latin for half a century and do not really know colloquial Latin. When my little daughter was four years old she lost faith in the wisdom of some Latin professors when talking with a Latin instructor who did not understand the salutation

'Quid agis' and gazed at her blankly when she spoke of the courses at the table *'ab ovo usque ad mala.'"*

Keeping in mind the child's remarkable ability to learn spoken language, let us stress again the fact that the process by which spoken language and written language is understood is precisely the same.

Then doesn't it follow that young children should also have a unique ability to read language? The fact is that, given an opportunity to do so, they do demonstrate such an ability. We shall shortly see some examples of this.

When a person or group is led by research to what appears to be a new and important idea, several things are necessary before duty compels that group to the publication and dissemination of this idea.

First the idea must be tested in life to see what the results of this idea being put into effect may be. They may be good or they may be bad or they may be indifferent.

Secondly, no matter how new such concepts may appear to be, it is possible that someone somewhere has had such ideas before and has used them. It is possible that they have somewhere reported their findings.

It is not only the privilege but, indeed, it is the

duty of people expressing such ideas to conduct a careful search of all available documents to determine what anyone else may have had to say on the subject. This is true even when it would appear to be an entirely new idea.

In the years between 1959 and 1962 our team was aware that other people were working with young children in the area of reading, both in and outside of the United States. We had a general idea of what they were doing and saying. While we agreed with much of what was being done and certainly that it was a good thing to do, we believed that the basis of such learning was neurological rather than psychological, emotional, or educational.

When we began to study the literature on the subject intensively we were impressed by four facts:

1. The history of teaching little children to read was not new and indeed stretches back for centuries.
2. Often people generations apart do the same things although for different reasons and different philosophies.
3. Those who had decided to teach young children to read had all used systems which, although they varied somewhat in technique, had many common factors.

4. *Most importantly, in all of the cases we were able to find where small children were taught to read in the home, everyone who tried had succeeded, no matter what the method.*

Many of the cases were carefully observed and recorded in detail. Few were clearer than the aforementioned case of little Winifred. Mrs. Stoner had come to almost the same conclusions about early reading as those of us at The Institutes, although she did so without the neurological knowledge available to us.

In *Natural Education,* Mrs. Stoner wrote:

"When my baby was six months old I placed a border of white cardboard four feet in height around the walls of her nursery. On one side of the wall I placed the letters of the alphabet, which I had cut from red glazed paper. On another wall I formed from the same red letters simple words arranged in rows as bat, cat, hat, mat, rat; bog, dog, hog, log. You will notice that there were only nouns in these lists...

"After Winifred had learned all of her letters I began to teach her the words on the wall by spelling them out and making rhymes about them...

"Through these games of word building, and the impressions made upon Winifred's mind by reading to her, she learned to read at the age of sixteen months, without having been given a so-called reading lesson. Four of my friends have tried this method and have met with success, as the children who were taught in this way all could read simple English text before they were three years old."

The story of this child and her friends learning to read is by no means unique.

In 1918 another remarkably similar example was reported. This was the case of a child named Martha (sometimes called Millie) whose father, an attorney, began to teach her to read when she was nineteen months old.

Martha lived near Lewis M. Terman, a famous educator. Terman was astonished by the success Martha's father achieved in teaching Martha and he urged her father to write a detailed account of what he had done. This account was published, with an introduction by Terman, in the *Journal of Applied Psychology*, Vol. II (1918).

Coincidentally, Martha's father also used large red block letters for his words as has the author, and as had Winifred's mother.

In writing of her in *Genetic Studies of Genius and Mental and Physical Traits of a Thousand Gifted Children (1925)* Terman said:

"This girl probably holds the world's record for early reading. At the age of twenty-six and a half months her reading vocabulary was above seven hundred words, and as early as twenty-one months she read and apprehended simple sentences as connected thoughts rather than as isolated words. By that age she could distinguish and name all the primary colors.

"By the time she was twenty-three months old she began to experience evident pleasure when she read. At twenty-four months she had a reading vocabulary of over two hundred words, which had increased to more than seven hundred words two and a half months later.

"When she was twenty-five months old she read fluently and with expression to one of us from several primers and first readers that she had never seen before. At this age her reading ability was at least equal to that of the average seven year old who had attended school a year."

In Philadelphia, The Institutes for the Achievement of Human Potential has found it possible to teach even brain-injured children to read well. This does not prove that such children are superior to unhurt children; it simply shows that very young children can learn to read.

And we adults really *should* permit them to do so, if for no other reason than the fact that they enjoy it so much.

4
tiny children
are learning
to read

It sounds silly to say that he can read when he's only three years old but when we go to market he reads the names on so many of the cans and packages.

—ALMOST ALL PARENTS
WHO HAVE A THREE-YEAR-OLD

In November of 1962, at a meeting of a group of educators, physicians, and others concerned with the neurological development of children, a county supervisor of education told the following story.

He had been an educator for thirty-five years. Two weeks before the meeting, a kindergarten teacher had reported that when she prepared to read a book to her five-year-olds, one of the children had volunteered to read it. The teacher pointed out that the book was a new one that the five-year-old had never seen, but he insisted that he could read it anyway. The teacher decided that the easiest way to dissuade the child was to let him try. She did—and he did. He read the entire book aloud to his class, accurately and easily.

The supervisor pointed out that for the first thirty-two years of his life as an educator he had occasionally heard stories about five-year-olds who could read books, but that in all of those three decades he had never actually seen one who could. However, he pointed out, in the last three years there had been at least one child in every kindergarten group who could read.

Thirty-two years of no five-year-olds who could read and then at least one in every one of his kindergartens for the last three years! The educator concluded by stating that he had investigated every case to determine who had taught these children to read.

"Do you know who had taught every one of these children to read?" he asked the child developmentalist who was leading the discussion.

"Yes," said the developmentalist, "I think I do know. The answer is that nobody taught them."

The supervisor agreed that this was the case.

In a sense nobody had taught these children to read, just as in a sense it is true that nobody teaches a child to understand spoken language. In a broader sense, everybody plus the child's environment had taught the child to read, just as everybody plus the child's environment teaches a child to understand spoken language.

Today television is a standard part of the environment of virtually all American children. This is the major factor which had been added to the lives of these kindergarten children.

By watching television commercials which show big clear words accompanied by loud clear pronunciations, children are unconsciously beginning to learn to read. By asking a few key questions of adults who are unaware of what is taking place, this ability to read has been expanded. By having children's books read to them by parents who are attempting only to amuse them, these children have attained astonishing reading vocabularies.

In the cases where parents have become aware of what was actually going on, they have delightedly aided the child in his learning. Generally they have done so despite dire but vague predictions by well-meaning friends that something awful but difficult to classify would happen to the child if they helped him to learn to read before he went to school.

Although we had made no public announcement of our work until mid-1963, there were hundreds of professional visitors to The Institutes as well as postgraduate students of The Institutes who, prior to 1963, were aware of our interest in teaching very young children to read.

In addition there were well over four hundred mothers and fathers of brain-injured children who were at various stages of teaching these children to read under our direction. More than one hundred of these brain-injured children ranged in age from one to five, while another hundred were six years of age and over.

It was inevitable that word of what we were doing should begin to leak out. By the beginning of 1963 we had received hundreds of letters. By the middle of 1963, following an article by the author in a national magazine, we had received thousands of letters.

A surprisingly small percentage of these letters were critical in nature and we shall deal later with those and the questions they raised.

Mothers wrote us letters from all over the United States and from many foreign countries. We were delighted and gratified to learn that a great many parents had taught two- and three-year-olds to read. In some cases they had done so fifteen or more years before. Many of the children so taught were now in college or had graduated. These letters constituted a flood of new evidence about the reading ability of young children.

Here are a few abstracts from some of the letters we received.

Dear Sirs:

...I thought you might be interested to hear that I did teach a baby to read seventeen years ago. I had no real system and in fact did not know at the time that this was very unusual. It came about through my enjoying books myself, reading to the child when she was very young and then being ill for several months so that I needed passive things to do with my two-and-a-half-year-old.

We had a game with letters two or three inches high, and cards with simple words on them. She took an intense interest in these letters, and in finding counterparts in our little books. She even learned some of the letters from sky-writing.

When the child was still of pre-kindergarten age she could read enough in the newspaper to find articles about fires, which scared her; and had certainly long passed primers...

She is now an honor student in a fine university and, further, a success socially and in sports, as well as in other lines of skills and interest. This is what lies ahead for at least one person who could read before she was three...

Dear Sir:

...I have seen it proved in my own daughter. She is now fifteen years old...a sophomore in high school, and has been a straight 'A' student since she was in first grade.

...She has a wonderful personality and is well liked by her teachers and the students...

My husband is a disabled veteran of World War I...Neither of us had enough education to hold a worthwhile job. He went to the fifth grade and I to the eighth. We made a living by traveling and selling small articles house to house... We bought an eighteen-foot trailer house... She was raised in that trailer... When my daughter was ten months old I bought her her first book...It was really an ABC book with the objects of what each letter stood for, A for apple, etc. In six months she knew every object and could name them. When she was two years old I got her a larger ABC book (and other books too). While we were traveling it was an excellent time for teaching her. While we were stopped in the different towns she needed something to occupy her mind. If I was selling, my husband had to keep her entertained. She always wanted to know what the different signs spelled...My husband would tell her...We never did teach her the alphabet. She learned that later on, in school...She was started in school on her sixth birthday in the first grade and it was no trouble at all for her to make A's...Oh yes, we still live in a trailer house, thirty-four feet long. One end is for her books... We have a city library here and she has made a big dent in their book supply.

I know this is a long letter and it may sound like bragging but really it isn't meant to be that. I know if young parents would only take the time, there are plenty of children who could do the same things that our daughter has done, if given the chance. You can't just jerk these kids up and plop them into school at the age of six and expect them to learn quickly, without a little foundation work from the time they are babies on up.

...If you think this letter would be of any help to young parents you may print it. If not, that is O.K. anyway. The main thing was I wanted you to know that I know, "You *Can* Teach Your Baby to Read!"

Gentlemen:

...I wish to add that it can be done by an uninformed amateur like myself ... my older one accidentally learned the alphabet before he was eighteen months old...

...about the time he was three he would ask what road signs meant. . . and he was reading before he was in kindergarten without much help from me except for answering his questions. Although he is now in first grade and learning to write neatly on that level, he is doing all second grade work in reading and arithmetic and is near the top of the class in these...does the high I.Q. come as the result of reading early, or does reading early come as the result of a high I.Q.?

...I have never had much time to talk with my second one, and as a result he is not nearly as scholarly...However, I can not help regretting the fact that I gave my second boy less attention in this respect and it may be a drawback all his life.

...I for one also say that they *love* to learn and can learn a great deal more at an early age when it is just "child's play" to them.

Dear Sir:

...finally giving recognition to the fact that children of two, three, and four years of age can be taught to read, and moreover, want to learn to read. My own daughter knew her complete alphabet...and could read several words at the age of two. A few days after her third birthday she suddenly, it seemed, realized that reading several words in succession produced that complete thought known as a sentence. From that time her reading has progressed rapidly and now, at four and a half, she reads at least as well as most children completing their second grade in school.

A medical doctor in Norway made these comments:

Dear Sir:

I have taught two of my three children to read at four and three years, by a slightly different method. Your arguments sound very convincing to me. From my experience I think your method definitely better than my own, and I will try to use it with my youngest child (seven months) next year.

...In Norway reading is kept from preschoolers as jealously as information about sex in earlier times. In spite of this I found the following results when I examined 200 preschoolers: ten percent were reading fairly well and more than a third knew all the letters.

I think developing the brain is the most important and challenging job of our time, and in my opinion you have done truly pioneering work.

It must be made clear that these mothers had taught their children to read, or had discovered that their children could read, before the publication of this book and should in no way be construed to be endorsements of the methods outlined in this book. They are simply letters from alert mothers who agree that children *can* learn to read, *are* learning to read, and *should* learn to read prior to entering school.

For many years, Dr. O.K. Moore did extensive research at Yale in how to teach preschool children to read. Dr. Moore found that it is easier to teach a three-year-old to read than a four-year-old, a four-year-old than a five-year-old, a five-year-old than a six-year-old.

Of course it's easier.

It should be.

Yet, how many times have we heard it said that children cannot learn to read until they are six—and that they should not?

In 1894, a woman named Maria Montessori was the first female to graduate from an Italian medical school. Dr. Montessori became interested in the highly neglected group of children who were loosely classified as "retarded." Such a classification is most unscientific, since there are hundreds of different reasons why a child's development may be held back. Nonetheless, Maria Montessori brought to this pathetically misunderstood group of children both a medical background and a womanly sympathy and appreciation.

Working with such children, she began to appreciate that they could be trained to perform at much higher levels than was at that time the case, and that this was particularly true if such training began earlier than at school age.

Dr. Montessori decided, over a period of years, that these children should be approached through all of the senses and began to teach them through visual, auditory, and tactile means. Her results were so gratifying that some of her "retarded" children began to do as well as some normal children. As a result Dr. Montessori concluded that well children were not performing anywhere near their potential and that they should be given an opportunity to do so.

Montessori schools have existed for many years in Europe for hurt children as well as for average children. Now there are Montessori schools in the United States, dedicated to helping well children of preschool age achieve their potential. Children are engaged in a broad program at three years of age, and usually the result is that the majority of them are reading words at four.

The oldest Montessori school in the United States is the Whitby School at Greenwich, Connecticut, and a visit to that school revealed a group of delightful, happy, well-adjusted children, learning to read and to perform other tasks which up to now have been considered advanced for preschool children.

One year after the reading program had been introduced at The Institutes, there were 231 brain-injured children learning to read. Of these children, 143 were below six years of age. The rest were six years or older, and could not read prior to the beginning of the program.

These children, who had physical problems as well as language problems, visited The Institutes every sixty days. On the occasion of each visit their neurological development was tested (including their reading ability). The parents were then taught the next step, as described later in this book, and were sent home to continue the physical program as well as the reading schedule.

By the time these *brain-injured* children had been on the program for periods ranging from one visit (sixty days) to five visits (ten months) *every child* could read something, ranging from letters of the alphabet to entire books. Many brain-injured three-year-olds in this group could read sentences and books with total understanding.

As has been said, the foregoing does not prove that brain-injured children are superior to well children, but simply that well children are not achieving what they can and should.

The figures cited do not include the hundreds of reading problems encountered at The Institutes by children who are not brain-injured but who are failing in school because they cannot read. Nor do they include the groups of well two- and three-year-old children whom their parents are teaching to read under the guidance of The Institutes.

At Yale University, as we have seen, Dr. Moore taught small children to read.

So have the Montessori schools.

So do The Institutes in Philadelphia.

It is quite possible that other groups, of whom the authors are unaware, are also purposely teaching tiny children to read, using an organized system.

In virtually all parts of the United States tiny children are learning to read even without their parents' guidance. As a result, we are going to have to make some decisions.

The first decision will have to be whether or not we *want* two- and three-year-old children to read.

If we decide we *don't* want them to be able to read, there are at least two things we have to do:

1. Do not read books, headlines, road signs, or product names to them.
2. Make certain they never see words shown on television, videos, or computers.

Now, on the other hand, if we don't want to go to all that trouble, we could take the easy way out and just go right ahead and let them read. If we do decide to take the easy way out and to permit little children to read, we certainly should do something about *what* they read.

We believe that the best way is to teach them to read at home with the parents' help rather than through television. It is easy, and the parents enjoy it almost as much as the children.

Whether children are learning to read or not isn't a theory which we may argue. It is a fact. The only question is what we are going to do about it.

5
tiny children
should learn
to read

Do you not know, then, that the beginning in every task is the chief thing, especially for any creature that is young and tender? For it is then that it is best molded and takes the impression that one wishes to stamp upon it.

—PLATO

Herbert Spencer said that the brain should not be starved any more than the stomach. Education should begin in the cradle, but in an interesting atmosphere. The man to whom information comes in dreary tasks along with threats of punishment is unlikely to be a student in after years, while those to whom it comes in natural forms, at the proper times, are likely to continue through life that self-instruction begun in youth.

We have already discussed several children who were successfully taught by their mothers and who later developed splendidly, but those are not examples from the professional literature.

Let's now examine the results of the case of Millie (Martha), reported by Lewis M. Terman later in the life of this child.

By the time Millie was twelve years and eight months old she was two years ahead of children her own age, being in the last half of the ninth grade. Terman reports:

"In the previous semester she was the only pupil in lower nine class of about 40 to make the high school honor roll.

"In our 1927-28 follow-up, the first thing the field visitor asked Millie's teacher was what subject she excelled in. The answer was, 'Millie reads beautifully.' In a chat with the field visitor Millie said she 'would like to read five books a day if it weren't for going to school.' She also admitted simply and without self-consciousness that she could read very fast, had read through Markham's thirteen volumes of the *Real American Romance* in a week. Her father, doubting whether she could read these books so rapidly and still assimilate them, asked her questions about the material read. She was able to answer them to his satisfaction."

Terman concludes that there is no evidence to indicate that Millie was in any way harmed by her being taught to read as a baby, and much evidence to support the view that her high abilities were due at least in part to her early training.

Her various I.Q test scores averaged to above 140, and she was strong and lively. She suffered no handicaps in social adaptability even though her classmates were two or three years her senior.

An I.Q. of 140 placed Millie in the genius category.

Many studies indicate that a very high number of superior adults and geniuses were able to read long before they went to school. It has always been assumed that these people could read at such a young age *because* they were superior people. This is a perfectly proper scientific premise and we have always accepted it.

However, in light of the many instances on record where parents have decided to teach tiny children to read long before it was possible to make a valid test of their intelligence, and therefore before there was any reason to assume that a child would be superior, we must now raise some new questions.

Is it not that these children became superior *because* they were taught to read at an early age?

The fact that there are so many superior persons, and indeed geniuses, who could read before they were of school age, supports either the first or second assumption equally well.

There is, however, more evidence to support the second premise than there is to support the first, and it too is a perfectly valid scientific supposition.

The assumption that many highly intelligent people could read at a very young age *because* they are geniuses rests essentially on a genetic basis and presumes that all such people are superior because they were genetically endowed with this potential.

We would not dispute the fact that there are genetic differences in people, nor would we care to become deeply involved with the age-old discussion of how much environment weighs when measured against genetics, since it does not directly concern the primary point of this book.

Still, we cannot close our eyes to the considerable evidence that supports the possibility that early reading has a strong influence on performance in later life.

1. Many children who turned out to be superior were taught to read before there was any evidence that they were in any way unusual. Indeed, some parents had decided before a child was born that they would make him superior by teaching the child to read at an early age, and did so.

2. In many of the recorded cases one child was

taught to read and later proved to be superior, while other children in the *same* family with the *same* parents were not taught to read early and did not become superior. In some cases the child taught to read was the first child. In other families, for various reasons, the child who learned to read early was not the first child.

3. In the case of Tommy Lunski (and there are other cases similar to his) there was certainly nothing to indicate that Tommy would have any special genetic endowment. Tommy's parents both have less than a high school education and are in no way intellectually unusual. Tommy's brothers and sisters are average children. In addition to all this, it should be recalled that Tommy was very severely brain-injured, and at two years of age it was recommended that he be placed in an institution for life as "hopelessly retarded." There is no question but that Tommy was an extraordinary child who read and comprehended at least as well as the average child more than twice his age.

Would it be fair, scientific, or even rational to refer to Tommy as a "gifted" child?

Thomas Edison said that genius is one percent inspiration and ninety-nine percent perspiration.

We have already discussed in some detail the six neurological functions which belong exclusively to human beings, and have pointed out that three of these are *receptive* abilities while the other three are *expressive.*

It seems obvious that man's intelligence is limited to the information he can gain from the world through his receptive senses. The highest of these receptive abilities is the ability to read.

It is equally obvious that if all three of man's receptive abilities were totally cut off, he would be more of a vegetable than a human being.

Man's intelligence, then, is limited by the sum of the three uniquely human characteristics of seeing and hearing in a manner that culminates in the ability to read and to understand spoken language, and a special ability to feel that enables him, if necessary, to read language by feeling.

Destroy these three receptive abilities and you destroy most of what makes man different from other animals.

Limit these three abilities and you will equally limit a human being's intelligence.

Unless one of these three human abilities is high, we will see a human being whose intelligence is affected.

If one of these abilities is higher than the others, the person will perform to the top level of that ability, *provided every conceivable opportunity is made available to that person to gain information through that single facility.*

No person will rise above the highest receptive ability he has plus the opportunity he is given to use that receptive ability.

The reverse is, of course, equally true. If all three of these abilities in a single human being are low, then that human being will perform at a very low level.

If we could imagine a situation in which man suddenly lost his ability to read and to hear language, it would be necessary to teach the new generation to communicate in some other way. It is obvious that we would choose the sense of touch to communicate, as did Helen Keller's first teacher, since her pupil, because of blindness and deafness, could not speak, read, or write. If Helen Keller's ability to receive language through the sense of touch had been very low, she could have existed only at an animal level. Had her sense of touch been nonexistent, as was her sight and hearing, she would have existed at a vegetable level.

When these capacities are increased in man, his ability to perform will be increased.

Certainly the severely brain-injured children who were taught to read at a very early age have demonstrated far greater ability than the brain-injured children who were not given such an opportunity. And the well children whose cases have been cited, and many others, appear to have performed at much higher levels than their peers who were not given such an opportunity.

It may be true that there are some brain-injured adults who can understand language in a limited way, but there are no geniuses who *cannot* understand language—not in our culture at any rate.

Of course it must be borne in mind that intelligence can only be related to the culture in which it exists. A normal adult Australian aborigine brought to New York City and given an ordinary American intelligence test would be found to be an idiot by our standards.

On the other hand, an adult American taken to a tribe of Australian aborigines would be almost helpless in that culture and would probably not even survive unless cared for by those people, much in the manner we care for our babies. Obviously the American would be unable to get food with a boomerang, unable to catch live lizards and eat them raw, unable to find water, and, particularly, unable to understand what he was being told—at least for a while.

Language is the most important tool available to man. Man can have no more sophisticated thoughts than he has language to formulate them. If he needs additional words, he must invent them to use as tools for thinking and communicating the new thought.

This is easily seen in our technical society, where thousands of words must be invented each decade to describe man's new devices. During World War II, the Fifth Air Force trained a large group of American Indians in radio techniques and sent them to units in the Pacific. Since few if any Japanese could speak Choctaw or Sioux, it was hoped that valuable time could be saved by not having to code messages.

It was found that there were simply no words in the Indian languages to describe a fighter bomber, a torpedo plane, an aircraft carrier, fuel injection, or countless other Air Force terms.

Virtually all tests of intelligence applied to human beings are dependent upon the ability to take in written information (reading) or upon the ability to take in spoken information. In our culture this is as it should be.

If the ability to read is reduced or nonexistent, there is no question that the ability to express intelligence is also markedly diminished.

While it is obvious that lack of material to read, or the lack of ability to read it, inevitably results in lack of education, it is infinitely more important that it also results in decreased opportunity to gain knowledge.

This could result in lowered intelligence.

Language ability is a vital tool. The ability to express intelligence is therefore related to the facility of the language with which one is dealing.

There is no truly valid test of I.Q. in children below the age of two and a half years. One can start applying the Stanford-Binet test to a child two and a half years old and achieve results that may prove generally valid later in life. As language ability increases, however, the tests that are applied become more valid.

Naturally, the language proficiency required of a child in I.Q. testing is higher each year. It is therefore clear that if a child's verbal competence is more advanced than that of other children of the same age, he will test, and be considered, more intelligent than the other children.

Tommy Lunski was classified as a hopeless idiot at two, *essentially because he could not talk* (and thus express his intelligence), while he was considered to be a superior child at five *because he could read superbly.*

It is completely clear that the ability to read, and at an early age, has much to do with the measurement of intelligence. In the end it matters little whether the ability to express intelligence is a valid test of intelligence itself—it is the test upon which intelligence is judged.

The earlier a child reads, the more he is likely to read and the better he reads.

Some of the reasons, then, that children should learn to read when they are very young are as follows:

1. The hyperactivity of the two- and three-year-old child is, in fact, the result of a boundless thirst for knowledge. If he is given an opportunity to quench that thirst, at least for a small part of the time, he will be far less hyperactive, far easier to protect from harm, and far better able to learn about the world when he is moving about and learning about the physical world and himself.
2. The child's ability to take in information at two and three years of age will never be equaled again.
3. It is infinitely easier to teach a child to read at this age than it will ever be again.
4. Children taught to read at a very young age absorb a great deal *more information* than do children whose early attempts to learn are frustrated.
5. Children who learn to read while very young

tend to comprehend better than youngsters who do not. It is interesting to listen to the three-year-old, who reads with inflection and meaning, in contrast to the average seven-year-old, who reads each word separately and without appreciation of the sentence as a whole.

6. Children who learn to read while very young tend to read much more rapidly and comprehensively than children who do not. This is because young children are much less awed by reading and do not consider it a "subject" full of frightening abstractions. Tiny children view it as just another fascinating thing in a world jammed with fascinating things to be learned. They do not "hang up" on the details but deal with reading in a totally functional sense. They are very right to do so.

7. *Finally, and at least as important as the above stated reasons—children love to learn to read at a very early age.*

6
who has problems, readers or nonreaders?

Many of these children are ordinarily classi-fied as gifted, but where records are adequate all precocious readers received a great deal of prior stimulation. Consequently, to label a child as gifted in no way dispenses with the necessity of stimulation ... if he is to learn.

—WILLIAM FOWLER, *Cognitive Learning in Infancy and Early Childhood*

There was a strong temptation to entitle this chapter "Something Awful Is Going to Happen," since its purpose is to cover the dire predictions concerning what will happen to youngsters who read too soon. It was also tempting to call this chapter "Nobody Listens to Mothers," which is at least part of the reason why so many myths arise about youngsters.

There is a myth abroad in the land which holds

that only experts of one kind or another understand children. Among the innumerable kinds of experts who deal with children there are too many who insist that:

1. Mothers don't know much about children;
2. Mothers are completely inaccurate observers of their own children;
3. Mothers tell awful lies about their own children's abilities.

In our own experience nothing could be further from the truth.

While we have met some mothers who tell fantastic and untrue stories about their children and who do not understand them, we think they are very rare indeed. Rather, we have found mothers to be careful and sound observers of their own children, and they are, besides, absolutely stark realists.

The trouble is that hardly anybody listens to mothers.

At The Institutes we teach more than a thousand parents of brain-injured children each year. There is hardly anything a mother fears more than having a brain-injured child. And if she suspects it, she wants to find out at the first possible moment so she can immediately start doing whatever has to be done.

In over nine hundred out of a thousand cases seen at The Institutes, it was Mother who first decided that *something* was wrong with her baby. In most cases Mother had a very difficult time convincing anyone—including the family doctor and other professional people—that something was wrong and that something should be done about it at that instant.

No matter how hard or how long everyone tries to talk her out of it she persists until the situation is recognized. Sometimes it takes her years. The more she loves her baby, the more detached she makes herself in evaluating the baby's condition. If the child has a problem, she will not rest until it is solved.

At The Institutes we have learned to listen to mothers.

However, when dealing with well children, many professionals have succeeded in thoroughly intimidating mothers. They have frequently managed to get mothers to parrot a great deal of professional jargon which is often not even understood. Worst of all, they have come close to blunting mothers' instinctive reactions to their growing children, convincing them that they are being betrayed by their maternal instincts.

If this trend continues, we run the serious risk of persuading mothers to view their offspring not as children at all but instead as little bundles of strange ego drives that an untrained mother couldn't possibly understand.

Nonsense. In our experience mothers make the very best mothers there are.

Nowhere have we jammed more myths and fears down mothers' throats, or forced mothers to thwart all their maternal instincts, than in the area of preschool learning.

Today many mothers have come to believe things which they think are true simply because they have been repeated so often. We shall try to deal seriously with these common statements, all of which are myths to one degree or another.

Myth #1: Children who read too early will have learning problems.

The Fact: In none of the children we know personally, nor in any of the children we have read about who were taught at home, have we found this to be the case. In fact, in the vast majority of the cases precisely the reverse is true. Many of the results of early reading have already been described.

It is difficult to understand why there is so much surprise over the fact that such a high percentage of children have a reading problem. It is not at all surprising. What is surprising is that *anyone* learns to read, starting as most do when the capacity to learn easily and naturally is just about over.

Myth #2: Children who read too early will be nasty little geniuses.

The Fact: Come, come, myth makers, let's get together. Are the early readers going to be dunces or geniuses? It's surprising, really, how often the same person will tell Myth #1 and also Myth #2. The fact is that neither is true.

Where we have seen early readers we have seen happy, well-adjusted children who had more to enjoy than other children. We do not hold that early reading will *solve* all of the problems which might beset a child, and we suppose if you looked far enough you might find a child who was an early reader and who for other reasons also happened to be a nasty kid. In our experience you would have to look further for such a child among the early readers than you would among those who learned to read in school. We are quite confident that you could find many, many unhappy and badly adjusted children among those who *cannot* read when they start school. They are very common indeed.

Myth #3: The child who reads too early will cause problems in first grade.

The Fact: This is not wholly a myth, for it is partly true. He will cause problems at first. Not for *him,* but for the teacher. Since schools are meant to be for the good of the child rather than for the teacher, it will be necessary for the teacher to exercise a bit of effort to solve her problem. Daily, hundreds of fine teachers are doing just that, with ease. It is the few teachers not willing to make a small degree of effort who are largely responsible for keeping this complaint in circulation. But any teacher worth her salt can handle the advanced reader with a fraction of the time and effort necessary to cope with the problems of the legion of kids who *can't* read. As a matter of fact, a first-grade teacher with a class full of children who can read and who love it would have relatively few problems. This situation would also solve many problems later on, since much time is spent in *all* grades dealing with nonreaders.

It's too bad that the first-grade teacher can't solve all of her problems (and she has dozens of them) as easily as she can cope with the child who can read when he arrives in first grade. Hundreds of good first-grade teachers solve this problem very simply by giving the child books to read by himself while she struggles through the alphabet with his classmates. Many teachers go further and actually have the child read aloud to his classmates. He generally enjoys the opportunity to demonstrate his ability, and the other children are less awed when they see that it can be done. Good teachers have many approaches to this "problem."

What do we do about unimaginative teachers? That is a problem, isn't it? It's a problem for *all* the children in any class that has a poor teacher. The chances are excellent that the following will happen when a first-grade class has such a teacher: The child who will be the best in second grade is the one who could read before he started school. He didn't need first grade nearly as much as the other children.

Ironically, even the school that objects the most to a child who can read before he enters first grade is extremely proud of a child who is a superior reader in the *second* grade. One of the easiest problems that any sensible first-grade teacher has to deal with is what to do with the child who *can* read. The most difficult problem for her, and the most time-consuming, is the child she *can't* teach to read.

Even if all this were not true, would anyone seriously argue that we should prevent a child from learning in order to keep him at the average level of his classmates?

Myth #4: The child who learns to read too early will be bored in first grade.

The Fact: This is the fear that concerns the vast majority of mothers and is the question that is most sensible of all. To state it more accurately, what we are really asking here is, "Won't the child who has learned *too much* be bored in first grade?"

The answer to this is that, yes, there is a good chance he'll be bored silly in first grade *just like almost every other kid in first grade.* Did the reader ever live through days half as long as those he spent in first grade? Schools by and large are much better today than they were when the reader of this book went to school. But ask almost any first grader how long a school day is as compared to Saturday or Sunday. Does his answer mean that he doesn't want to learn? Not at all, but when five-year-olds carry on the sophisticated conversations that they do, can we really expect them to get very pepped up when they read such enduring material as "See the automobile. It is a pretty red automobile." The seven-year-old who has to read such sentences cannot only see the pretty red automobile, he can tell you the manufacturer, the year, the body type, and probably the horsepower. If there is anything else you'd like to know about the pretty red automobile, just ask him. He knows more about it than you do. Children will go right on being bored in school until we give them material worthy of their interest.

To assume that the child who knows the most will be the most bored is to assume that the child who knows the least is the most interested and therefore the least bored. If the class is uninteresting, all will be bored. If it is interesting, only the ones who are not able to understand will be bored.

Myth #5: The child who learns to read too early will miss phonetics.

The Fact: He may miss phonetics, but if he does he won't miss it. The foregoing may be a bad play on words, but it is a fact.

Dr. O.K. Moore, who has been mentioned previously as one of the true pioneers in teaching three-year-olds to read, refused to be drawn into the perpetual and extremely peripheral battle which rages in the controversy between the advocates of the "look-say" approach to reading and the "phonics" approach to reading. He has termed this a sterile fight.

At the present time there is no "best" way to teach very young children to read. There is certainly no exclusive method, any more than there is one to teach a child to learn language through his ear. You might well ask yourself, "Did I teach my child to hear by the 'phonics' method or the 'listen-hear' method, or did I simply expose him to spoken language?" You might ask also, "How well did he do?" If he learned to hear and speak language fairly well, maybe the system you used was a pretty good system.

The materials which we at The Institutes use to help tiny children to learn to read contain no black magic, or red magic either. They are simply a neat, orderly, organized approach to teaching a child how to read. They are based on an understanding of how a child's brain grows and on experience with a great many normal as well as hurt children. They are simply *a* way that has the virtue of working with a very high percentage of tiny children.

Yes, it's true. Your child may miss phonics

if you teach him to read when he's tiny—and won't that be nice.

Myth #6: The child who reads too early will have a reading problem.

The Fact: He may, but his chances will be far smaller of having a reading problem than they will be if he learns to read at the usual time.

Children who *can* read don't have reading problems. Those who *can't* read have the problems.

Myth #7: The child who reads too early will be deprived of his precious childhood.

The Fact: Of all the taboos which have been built up around children and reading this is the most patent piece of nonsense. Let's look at life for a minute and examine the facts, not a group of illusory fairy tales.

Is the average two- or three-year-old child occupied every minute of the day, having the most delightful time doing what he enjoys more than anything else? What he likes the most is spending every possible minute at work and play with his family. Nothing, just nothing, can compare with his family's undivided attention, and if he had his way that's the way he'd arrange it.

But what child in our society, our culture, and our time ever has such a childhood? Little practical details keep interfering. Details like: Who is going to clean the house, who is going to do the laundry, who is going to do the ironing, who is going to cook the dinner, who is going to do the dishes, who is going to do the shopping? In most homes that we know of—contrary to the modern notion—it is *still* Mom who does these things.

A clever mother and a patient mother can find ways to do some of these things with her two-year-old, like introducing him to the wonderful game of doing the dishes. When she does this, it is an elegant thing to do.

However, the vast majority of the mothers we know have not been able to share all their chores with their children. The result of all this is that the average two-year-old who is lucky enough to be in his mother's care spends a high percentage of his time screaming in anguish to get out of the playpen. Mother simply had to put him there so that he wouldn't electrocute himself, get crushed, cut himself, or fall out the window while she got something done.

Is this the precious childhood we're talking

about wasting while he learns to read? It is, more or less, in practically every home we know. If it isn't the case in *your* home, and you are one of the people who can and does give your attention almost every moment of the day to your two-year-old, then we think you have nothing to worry about and that there is a good chance your two-year-old already knows how to read. You can't spend all day, every day, teaching him to play patty cake.

We haven't met a single mother, no matter how busy, who doesn't make it a point to find some time to spend with her child during every day of the child's early years. The question is how to spend that time most fruitfully, most happily, and most usefully. Certainly it's true that we don't want to waste a minute that will help to create a happier, more capable, more creative child.

We who have spent our lives as staff members of an organization which deals with the development of children are persuaded that there is no more productive and joyful way for mother and tiny child to occupy a few minutes together each day than in the pursuit of reading.

The joy that parent and child know as the child learns what words, sentences, and books mean has no parallel. This is one of the great fulfillments of a truly precious childhood.

Let us conclude by returning to Millie and her parents. In his published account of Millie, her father stated part of the case correctly and succinctly when he said, "If learning to read had not occupied the baby's mind, some other less fruitful activity would have."

But Millie's mother, exercising her female prerogative, had the last and perhaps most important word: "We enjoy each other so much that we don't seem to care about having others along, but I'm afraid it's rather selfish of us."

Myth #8: The child who reads too early will suffer from "too much pressure."

The Fact: If this myth means that it is possible to bring too much pressure on a child by teaching him to read, then it is certainly true. It is equally true that we can put too much pressure on a child by teaching him anything else.

Pressuring a child for any reason is a foolish thing to do and we urgently advise all parents against it. So don't. Now the question here is, what does pressuring have to do with providing a child with an opportunity to learn to read? If the reader decides that he or she would like to follow the advice contained in this book, the answer is that there is no connection between pressure and how a child should learn to read. Indeed, we not only advise parents *not* to pressure their children but insist that unless *both* parent and child are in the right frame of mind and eager to read, the child should not even be *permitted* to read.

There are probably a great number of additional ghost stories about the awful things that will happen if you teach a tiny child to read, but in all of our experience we have never seen one single unhappy result. All of the dire predictions we have heard are based on the lack of understanding of the process of brain development, of which reading should be a part.

In line with this, we might reiterate one of the most important points that this book seeks to make. Simply stated, and from a neurological standpoint, reading is not a school subject at all: It is a brain function.

Reading language is a brain function exactly as hearing language is a brain function.

What would our reaction be if, in examining a child's classroom subjects, we found geography, spelling, civics, and hearing?

Surely we would say, what is hearing doing there, listed as a school subject? Hearing, we would surely say, is something the brain does, not to be confused with subjects taught in school.

So is reading.

Spelling, on the other hand, *is* a proper school subject.

A child may be a splendid reader and not necessarily a good speller. They are two different things and two totally diverse processes. Reading is something the brain does, and spelling is a subject about certain rules people have invented to help keep reading and writing orderly. When the teacher teaches spelling, she is passing on facts from the body of knowledge which man has accumulated. When a child reads, his brain is not dealing with the details of how a word is constructed. The child's brain is actually interpreting thoughts, expressed by the writer.

Let the reader ask himself two questions:

1. Can he read any words he is unable to spell? Of course he can—many.
2. Can he spell any words he cannot read? Of course he cannot.

    Reading is a brain function, and spelling is a set of rules. Just as we can read and understand words that we can't spell, we can even read and understand words that we cannot pronounce.

The authors recently heard a learned professor with a Ph.D. mispronounce the word "epitome." He had obviously been using the word for years and using it correctly. Even if he had been trained phonetically (and he probably had been), he would still have mispronounced this word. He had simply learned it by reading, as we learn the vast majority of the roughly one hundred thousand words that compose a decent vocabulary.

How many of those words were we actually *taught* in school? Only a small percentage. We come to school with a tremendous speaking vocabulary. We are taught to read, at the most, a few thousand words, and to spell, at the most, a few thousand more. The remaining tens of thousands we have come to know, we have taught ourselves by listening, by reading and, very occasionally, by looking some up in the dictionary.

By all of the above, do we mean to imply that we are opposed to children learning how to spell?

Of course not. Spelling is a very proper subject for school and a most important one.

Perhaps, one day in the future, everyone will come to the conclusion that young children should learn to read at home just as they presently learn to hear at home. What a blessing that would be for the privileged mother, for the fortunate child, for the terribly overworked teacher (who could then spend her time transmitting to her pupils the superb store of knowledge man has accumulated). And what a blessing it would also be for our under-financed, underhoused, understaffed school systems.

Look around and see who are the *real* problems in school.

Look at the ten top children in each class in school and see what common factor is the most prominent in the group. That's easy—they are the best readers.

The *nonreading* children are the greatest problem in American education.

7
how to teach your baby to read

We mothers are the potters and our children the clay.

—WINIFRED SACKVILLE STONER,
Natural Education

Most sets of instructions begin by saying that unless they are followed precisely, they won't work.

In contrast to that, it is almost safe to say that no matter how poorly you expose your baby to reading, he is almost sure to learn more than he would if you hadn't done it; so this is one game which you will win to some degree no matter how badly you play it. You would have to do it incredibly badly to produce no result.

Nonetheless, the more cleverly you play the game of teaching your tiny child to read, the more quickly and the better he will learn to read.

If you play correctly the game of learning to read, both you and your child will enjoy it immensely.

It takes less than a half-hour a day.

Let's review the cardinal points to remember about the child himself before discussing how to teach him to read.

1. The child below the age of five can easily absorb tremendous amounts of information. If the child is below four it will be easier and more effective, below three even easier and much more effective, and below two is the easiest and most effective of all.
2. The child below five can accept information at a remarkable rate.
3. The more information a child absorbs below the age of five, the more he retains.
4. The child below five has a tremendous amount of energy.
5. The child below five has a monumental desire to learn.

6. The child below five can learn to read and wants to learn to read.
7. The child below five learns an entire language and can learn as many languages as are presented to him. He can learn to read one language or several just as readily as he understands the spoken language.

TEACHING BASICS

At What Age to Begin

The question as to when to begin to teach a child to read is a fascinating one. When is a child ready to learn anything?

Once a mother asked a famous child developmentalist at what age she should begin to teach her child.

"When," he asked, "will your child be born?"

"Oh, he is five years old now," said the mother.

"Madam, run home quickly. You have wasted the best five years of his life," said the expert.

Beyond two years of age, reading gets harder every year. If your child is five, it will be easier than it would if he were six. Four is easier still, and three is even easier.

One year of age or younger is the best time to

begin if you want to expend the least amount of time and energy in teaching your child to read. You can really begin the process of teaching your baby right from birth. After all, we speak to the baby at birth—this grows the auditory pathway. We can also provide language through the eye—this grows the visual pathway.

There are two *vital* points involved in teaching your child:

1. Your attitude and approach.
2. The size and orderliness of the reading matter.

Parent Attitude and Approach

Learning is the greatest adventure of life. Learning is desirable, vital, unavoidable, and, above all, life's greatest and most stimulating game. The child believes this and will always believe this—unless we persuade him that it isn't true.

The cardinal rule is that both parent and child must joyously approach learning to read as the superb game that it is. The parent must never forget that learning is life's most exciting game—it is not work. Learning is a reward; it is not a punishment. Learning is a pleasure; it is not a chore. Learning is a privilege; it is not denial.

The parent must always remember this and she must never do anything to destroy this natural attitude in the child.

There is a fail-safe law you must never forget. It is this: If you aren't having a wonderful time and your child isn't having a wonderful time—stop. You are doing something wrong.

The Best Time to Teach

Mother must never play this game unless she *and* her child are happy and in good form. If a child is irritable, tired, or hungry it is not a good time to do the reading program. If Mother is cranky or out of sorts, this is not a good time to do the reading program. On a bad day it is best not to play the reading game at all. Every mother and child experiences days when they are at odds or things just don't seem to be going smoothly. It is a wise mother who puts away her reading program on such days, recognizing full well that there are many more happy days than cranky ones and that the joy of learning to read will be enhanced by choosing the very best and happiest moments to pursue it.

Never try to teach a child anything when he is tired or hungry or upset. Find out what is bothering him and handle it. Then you can get back to the joy of teaching him to read and having a great time together.

The Best Duration

Make sure that the length of time you play the game is very short. At first it will be played three times a day, but each session will involve only a few seconds.

In regard to determining when to end each session of learning, the parent should exercise great foresight.

Always stop before your child wants to stop.

The parent must know what the child is thinking a little bit before the child knows it, and must stop.

If the parent always observes this fact, the child will beg the parent to play the reading game and the parent will be nurturing rather than destroying the child's natural desire to learn.

The Manner of Teaching

Whether a reading session consists of five single words, sentences, or a book, your enthusiasm is the key. Children love to learn and they do it *very quickly.* Therefore you must show your material *very quickly.* We adults do almost everything too slowly for children and there is no area where this is more painfully demonstrated than the way adults teach little children. Generally we expect a child to sit and stare at his materials, to look as if he is concentrating on them. We expect him to look a bit unhappy in order to demonstrate that he is really learning. But children don't think learning is painful, grown-ups do.

When you show your cards, do so as fast as you can. You will become more and more expert at this as you do it. Practice a bit with Father until you feel comfortable. The materials are carefully designed to be large and clear so that you can show them very quickly and your child will see them easily.

Sometimes when a mother speeds up she is apt to become a bit mechanical and lose the natural enthusiasm and "music" in her voice. It *is* possible to maintain enthusiasm *and* good meaningful sound *and* go very quickly all simultaneously. It is important that you do. Your child's interest and enthusiasm for his reading sessions will be closely related to three things:

1. The speed at which materials are shown.
2. The amount of new material.
3. The joyous manner of Mother.

This point of speed, all by itself, can make the difference between a successful session and one that is too slow for your very eager, bright child.

Children don't stare—they don't *need* to stare—they absorb and they do so instantly, like sponges.

Introducing New Material

It is wise at this point to talk about the rate at which each individual child should learn to read or, for that matter, to learn anything.

John Ciardi, writing in the May 11, 1963, issue of *Saturday Review* said that a child should be fed new knowledge "at the rate determined by her own happy hunger."

This, I think, sums up the situation beautifully.

Don't be afraid to follow your child's lead.

You may be astonished at the size of his happy hunger and at the rate at which he learns.

We were raised in a world that taught us that one must learn twenty words perfectly. We must learn and be tested at 100 percent or else.

Instead of 100 percent of twenty, how about 50 percent of two-thousand? You don't need to be a mathematical genius to know that one-thousand words are a great deal more than twenty. But the real point here is not merely the fact that children can hold fifty times more than we offer them. The important point is what happens when you show the twenty-first word or the two-thousand-and-first word. This is where the secret of teaching very young children lies.

In the former case the effect of the introduction of the twenty-first word (when a child has seen the first twenty *ad infinitum* and *ad nauseam)* will be to send him running in the opposite direction as fast as possible. This is the basic principle that is followed in formal education. We adults are experts on how deadly this approach can be. We lived through twelve years of it.

In the latter case the two-thousand-and-first word is eagerly awaited. The joy of discovery and learning something new is honored and the natural curiosity and love of learning which is born in every child is fed as it should be.

Sadly, one method closes the door on learning—sometimes forever. The other opens the door wide and secures it against future attempts to close it.

In fact your child will learn a great deal more than 50 percent of what you teach. It is more than likely that he will learn 80 to 100 percent. But if he only learned 50 percent because you offered him so much he would be intellectually happy and healthy.

And after all, isn't that the point?

Consistency

It is wise to organize yourself and your materials before you begin because once you begin you will want to establish a consistent program. A modest program done consistently and happily will be infinitely more successful than an over-ambitious program that overwhelms Mother and therefore occurs very sporadically. An on-again-off-again program will not be effective. Seeing the materials repeatedly is vital to mastering them. Your child's enjoyment is derived from real knowledge and this can best be accomplished with a program done daily.

However, sometimes it *is* necessary to put the program away for a few days. This is no problem as long as it does not occur too often. Occasionally it may be vital to put it away for several weeks or even months. For example, a new baby's arrival, moving, traveling, or an illness in the family causes major disruptions to any daily routine. During such upheavals it is best to put your program away *completely*. Use this time to read to your child, which requires nothing more than a trip to the library once a week and a quiet reading time daily. Do not try to do a halfway program during these times. It will be frustrating for you and your child.

When you are ready to go back to a consistent program start back exactly where you left off. Do not go back and start over again.

Whether you decide to do a modest reading program or an extensive program, do whatever suits you *consistently*. You will see your child's enjoyment and confidence grow daily.

Material Preparation

The materials used in teaching your child to read are extremely simple. They are based on many years of work on the part of a very large team of child brain developmentalists who studied how the human brain grows and functions. They are designed in complete recognition of the fact that reading is a *brain* function. They recognize the capabilities and limitations of the tiny child's visual apparatus and are designed to meet all of his needs from visual crudeness to visual sophistication and from brain function to brain learning.

All materials should be made on fairly stiff white posterboard so that they will stand up under the not-always-gentle handling they will receive.

You will need a good supply of white posterboard cut into large strips, approximately 6" x 22" (15.24 cm x 55.88 cm). If possible, purchase these already cut to the size you want. This will save you a lot of cutting, which is much more time-consuming than writing words. Don't become obsessed over the exact size of these cards, but consider what size posterboard is available where you live and use common sense.

You will also need a large, red, felt-tipped marker. Get the widest tip available—the fatter the marker the better.

Now write each of the words on a white posterboard strip. Make the letters 3" high. Use lower-case letters except in the case of a proper noun, which, of course, always begins with a capital letter. Otherwise you will always use lowercase lettering since this is the way words appear in books.

Make certain your letters are very bold. The stroke should be approximately ½" wide or wider. This intensity is important to help make it easier for your child to see the word.

Make your lettering neat and clear. Use print, never cursive writing. Make sure you place the word on the card so that there is a border of ½" or more all around the word. This will give you space for your fingers when you hold up the card.

Sometimes mothers get very fancy and use stencils to make their cards. This makes very beautiful reading cards; however, the time involved is prohibitive. Your time is precious. Mothers have to budget time more carefully than members of almost any other profession. You need to develop a fast, efficient means of making your reading cards because you are going to need a *lot* of them. Neatness and legibility are far more important than perfection.

Mothers and fathers often share the job of making word cards, so try to be consistent about how you print. Again, your child needs the visual information to be consistent and reliable. This helps him enormously.

On the back of the card, print the word again in the upper left corner. Make this whatever size is easy for you to see and read.

You may use pencil or pen to do this. You will need this when you are teaching. Otherwise you will have to look at the front of each card first before showing your child the card; this is distracting and will slow down the speed of showing words.

The materials begin with large, red, lower-case letters and progressively change to normal-size, black, lower-case letters. They are large initially because the immature visual pathway cannot distinguish small print and it actually grows by use. The size can and should be reduced as the pathway matures.

The large letters are used initially for the very simple reason that they are most easily seen. They are red simply because red attracts a small child. To start out you may find it simpler to buy a ready-made kit. Information about purchasing the Glenn Doman *How To Teach Your Baby To Read* Kit is found at the back of this book.

Once you begin to teach your child to read, you will find that your child goes through new material very quickly. No matter how often we emphasize this point with parents, they are always astonished at how quickly their children learn.

We discovered a long time ago that it is best to start out ahead. For this reason, make at least two hundred words before you actually begin to teach your child. Then you will have an adequate supply of new material on hand and ready to use. If you do not do this, you will find yourself constantly behind. The temptation to keep showing the same old words over and over again looms large. If Mother succumbs to this temptation it spells disaster for her reading program. The one mistake a child will not tolerate is to be shown the same material over and over again after it should long since have been retired.

Remember, the cardinal sin is to bore the tiny child.

Be smart—start ahead in material preparation and stay ahead. And if for some reason you do get behind in preparing new materials, do not fill in the gap by showing the same old words again. Stop your program for a day or a week until you have reorganized and made new material, then begin again where you left off.

Material preparation can be a lot of fun and should be. If you are preparing next month's materials, it will be. If you are preparing tomorrow morning's materials, it will not be.

Start out ahead, stay ahead, stop, and reorganize if you must, but don't show old materials over and over again.

SUMMARY: THE BASICS OF GOOD TEACHING

1. Begin as young as possible.
2. Be joyous at all times.
3. Respect your child.
4. Teach only when you and your child are happy.
5. Stop before your child wants to stop.
6. Show materials quickly.
7. Introduce new materials often.
8. Do your program consistently.
9. Prepare your materials carefully and stay ahead.
10. Remember the Fail-Safe Law.

THE READING PATHWAY

The path that you will now follow in order to teach your child is amazingly simple and easy. Whether you are beginning with an infant or a four-year-old the path is essentially the same. The steps of that path are as follows:

First Step	Single words
Second Step	Couplets
Third Step	Phrases
Fourth Step	Sentences
Fifth Step	Books

THE FIRST STEP—*Single Words*

The first step in teaching your child to read begins with the use of just fifteen words. When your child has learned these fifteen words he is ready to progress to the vocabularies themselves.

Begin at a time of day when the child is receptive, rested, and in a good mood.

Use a part of the house with as few distracting factors as possible, in both an auditory and a visual sense; for instance, do *not* have on the radio or television, and avoid other sources of noise. Use a corner of a room that does not have a great deal of furniture, pictures, or other objects that might distract the child's vision.

Now the fun begins. Simply hold up the word *Mommy*, just beyond his reach, and say to him clearly, "This says *Mommy.*"

Give your child no more description. There is no need to elaborate. Permit him to see it for no more than one second.

Next, hold up the word *Daddy* and again with great enthusiasm say, "This says *Daddy.*"

Show three other words in precisely the same way as you have the first two. It is best when showing a set of cards to take the card from the back of the set rather than feeding from the front card. This allows you to glance at the upper left corner of the back of each card where you have written the word. This means that as you actually say the word to your child you can put your full attention on his face. This is ideal because you want to have your full attention and enthusiasm directed toward him rather than looking at the front of the card as he looks at it. *Do not ask* your child to repeat the words as you go along. After the fifth word, give your child a huge hug and kiss and display your affection in the most obvious ways. Tell him how wonderful and bright he is.

Repeat this three times during the first day, exactly as described above. Take a break between sessions (at least 15 minutes). Make sure the cards are in a different order each time.

The first day is now over and you have taken the first step in teaching your child to read. (You have invested at most three minutes.)

The second day, repeat the basic session three times. Add a second set of five new words. This new set should be seen three times throughout the day, just like the first set, making a total of six sessions.

At the end of each session tell your child he is very good and very bright. Tell him that you are very proud of him and that you love him very much. It is wise to hug him and to express your love for him physically.

Do not bribe him or reward him with cookies, candy, or the like. At the rate he will be learning in a very short time, you will not be able to afford enough cookies from a financial standpoint, and he will not be able to afford them from a health standpoint. Besides, cookies are a meager reward for such a major accomplishment, compared with your love and respect.

Children learn at lightning speed—if you show them the words more than three times a day you will bore them. If you show your child a single card for more than a second you will lose him. Now simply say the name of each word as you show it, without saying "This says...".

On the third day, add a third set of five new words. Now you are teaching your child three sets of reading words, five words in each set, each set three times a day. You and your child are now enjoying a total of nine reading sessions spread out during the day, equaling a few minutes in all.

The first fifteen words that you teach your child should be made up of the most familiar and enjoyable words around him. These words should include the names of immediate family members, relatives, family pets, favorite foods, objects in the house, and favorite activities. It is impossible to include an exact list here since each child's first fifteen words will be personal and therefore different.

The only warning sign in the entire process of learning to read is boredom. *Never bore your child. Going too slowly is much more likely to bore him than going too quickly.* Remember that this bright baby can be learning, say, Portuguese at this time, so don't bore him. Consider the splendid thing you have just accomplished. Your child has just conquered the most difficult thing he will have to do in the entire business of reading—and perhaps in the entire business of learning, since reading is the very basis of learning.

He has done, with your help, two most extraordinary things:

1. He has grown his visual pathway and, more important, taught his brain to differentiate between one written symbol and another.
2. He has mastered one of the most staggering abstractions he will ever have to deal with in life: he can read words.

A word about the alphabet. Why have we not begun by teaching this child the alphabet? The answer to this question is most important.

It is a basic tenet of all teaching that it should begin with the known and the concrete, progress from this to the new and the unknown, and last of all, to what is abstract.

Nothing could be more abstract to the two-year-old brain than the letter *b*. It is a tribute to the genius of children that they ever learn it.

It is obvious that if the two-year-old were only more capable of reasoned argument he would long since have made this situation clear to adults.

If such were the case, when we presented him with the letter b, he would ask, "Why is that thing *b*?"

What would we answer?

"Well," we would say, "it is *b* because...uh... because, don't you see it's *b* because...well,

because it was necessary to invent the....ah...
symbol to...ah...stand for the sound *b* which
...ah...we also invented so that...ah... "

And so it would have gone.

In the end most of us would surely say, "It's *b*
because I'm bigger than you, that's why it's *b.* "

And perhaps that's as good a reason as any
why *b* is *b.*

Happily, we haven't had to explain it to the
kids because, while perhaps they could not understand historically why *b* is *b,* they do know
that we are bigger than they are, and they
would feel this reason to be sufficient.

At any rate, they have managed to learn these
twenty-six visual abstractions and, what is more,
twenty-six auditory abstractions to go with
them.

This does not add up to fifty-two possible
combinations of sound and picture but instead
to an almost infinite number of possible combinations.

All this they learn even though we usually
teach them at five or six, when it's getting a lot
harder for them to learn.

Thank goodness we are wise enough not to
try to start law students, medical students, or
engineering students with any such wild abstractions, because, being young grownups,
they would never survive it.

What your youngster has managed in the first step, *visual differentiation,* is very important.

Reading letters is not nearly as much fun as reading words, since nobody ever ate a *b* or caught a *b* or wore a *b* or opened a *b*. One can eat a *banana,* catch a *ball,* swing a *bat,* or open a *book.* While the letters that make up the word *ball* are abstract, the ball itself is not and thus it is easier to learn the word *ball* than it is to learn the letter *b*.

Also the word *ball* is much more different from the word *nose* than the letter *b* is different from the letter *c*.

These two facts make words much easier to read than letters.

The letters of the alphabet are *not* the units of reading and writing any more than isolated sounds are the units of hearing and speaking. *Words* are the units of language. Letters are simply technical construction materials within words, as clay, wood, and rock are construction materials of a building. It is the bricks, boards, and stones that are the true units of house construction.

Much later, when the child reads well and is ready to write, we will teach him the alphabet. By that time he will be able to see why it was necessary for man to invent an alphabet and why we need letters.

We begin teaching a small child to read words

by using his name, the names of his family, and the "self" words because the child learns first about his own family and his body. His world begins inside and works gradually outside, a fact educators have known for a long time.

A number of years ago an intelligent child developmentalist expressed through some magic letters something that did much to improve education. These letters were V.A.T.—visual, auditory, and tactile. It was pointed out that children learned through a combination of seeing (V), hearing (A), and feeling (T). And yet mothers have always been playing and saying things like, "This little piggy went to market and this little piggy stayed home," holding the toes up so the child can see them (visual), saying the words so the child can hear them (auditory), and squeezing the toes so the child can feel them (tactile).

In any event, we begin with the family and the "self" words. These include *Parts of the Body.*

hand	hair	leg	shoulder
knee	toes	eye	bellybutton
foot	ear	mouth	finger
head	arm	elbow	teeth
nose	thumb	lips	tongue

Here is the method you should use from this point on in adding new words and taking out old ones: simply remove one word from each set that has already been taught for five days and replace the word with a new one in each set. Your child's first three sets have already been seen for a week so you may now begin to take out an old word in each set and put in a new one each day. Five days from now, retire an old word from each of the two sets you have just added in. From this point on, you should add one new word to each set daily and put away an old word. We call this process of putting away an old word, "retirement." However every retired word will later be called back to active duty when we get to the *second, third, fourth,* and *fifth steps,* as you will see shortly.

Mothers find that if they write the date in pencil on the back of the reading card they can easily tell which words have been shown longest and are ready to be retired.

When this system is working smoothly, gradually add a fourth set of words and then a fifth set of words to your daily program. Continue to retire one old word and add one new word to each set, as described above.

```
                    DAILY PROGRAM
Daily Content:      5 sets
One Session:        1 set (5 words) shown once
Frequency:          3 x daily each set
Intensity:          3-inch red words
Duration:           5 seconds
New Words:          5 daily (1 in each set)
Retired Words:      5 daily (1 from each set)
Life Span
of Each Word:       3 x daily for 5 days = 15 x
Principle:          Always stop before your
                    child wants to stop.
```

In summary, you will be teaching twenty-five words daily, divided into five sets of five words each. Your child will be seeing five new words daily or one new word in each set, and five words will be retired each day.

Avoid presenting consecutively two words that begin with the same letter. *Hair, hand,* and *head* all begin with *h* and therefore should not be taught consecutively. Occasionally a child will leap to the conclusion that *hair* is *hand* because the words both begin with *h* and are similar in appearance. Children who have already been taught the entire alphabet are much more likely to commit this error than children who do not know the alphabet. Knowing the alphabet causes minor confusion to the child. In teaching the word *arm*, for example, mothers may experience the problem of a child's recognizing his old friend *a* and exclaiming over it, instead of reading the word *arm*.

Again one must remember the supreme rule of never boring the child. If he is bored there is a strong likelihood that you are going too slowly. He should be learning quickly and pushing you to play the game some more.

If you have done it well he will be averaging five new words daily. He may average ten new words a day. If you are clever enough and enthusiastic enough, he may learn more.

When your child has learned the "self" words, you are ready to move to the next step in the process of reading. He now has *two* of the most difficult steps in learning to read behind him. If he has succeeded up to now, you will find it difficult to prevent him from reading much longer.

By now both parent and child should be approaching this game of reading with great pleasure and anticipation. Remember, you are building into your child a love of learning that will multiply throughout his life. More accurately, you are reinforcing a built-in rage for learning that will not be denied, but which can certainly be twisted into useless or even negative channels in a child. Play the game with joy and enthusiasm. Now you are ready to add nouns that are the familiar objects in your child's environment.

The Home Vocabulary

The "home" vocabulary consists of those words that name the objects common in your household: the objects in your house, the foods, and the animals.

By this time the child will have a reading vocabulary of twenty-five to thirty words. At this point there is sometimes the temptation to review old words over and over again. Resist this temptation. Your child will find this boring. Children love to learn new words but they do not love to go over and over old ones. You may also be tempted to test your child. Again, do not do this. Testing invariably introduces tension into the situation on the part of the parent, and children perceive this readily. They are likely to associate tension and unpleasantness with learning. We will discuss testing in greater detail in the next chapter.

Be sure to show your child how much you love and respect him at every opportunity.

Reading sessions should always be a time of laughter and physical affection. They become the perfect reward for you and your child for all the hard work you have both done.

Objects

chair	table	door
window	wall	bed
bathtub	stove	refrigerator
television	sofa	toilet

This list should also be added to or subtracted from, to reflect the child's home surroundings and family-owned items that are special to his particular family.

Now continue to feed your child's happy hunger with the "possessions" words.

Possessions (things that belong to the child himself)

truck	blanket	socks
cup	spoon	pajamas
shoes	ball	tricycle
toothbrush	pillow	bottle

Foods

juice	milk	orange
bread	water	carrot
butter	egg	apple
banana	potato	strawberry

Animals

elephant	giraffe	hippopotamus
whale	gorilla	dinosaur
rhinoceros	spider	dog
tiger	snake	fox

As in the previous categories, these lists should be altered to reflect your child's own particular possessions and those things he or she loves the most.

Obviously, the list will vary somewhat depending upon whether your child is twelve months old or five years old.

Your child is taught the words in exactly the same way he has been taught up to now. This list can vary from ten words to fifty words, as the parent and the child choose.

The reading list (which up to this point may be approximately fifty words) has been composed entirely of nouns. The next grouping in the home vocabulary reflects action and consequently introduces verbs for the first time.

Actions

drinking	sleeping	reading
eating	walking	throwing
running	jumping	swimming
laughing	climbing	creeping

For added fun with this set, as each new word is taught Mother first illustrates the act by (for example) jumping, and saying, "Mommy is jumping." She then has the child jump and says, "You are jumping." Mother now shows her child the word and says, "This word says *jumping*." In this way she goes through all the "action" words. The child will particularly enjoy this, since it involves him, his mother (or father), action, and learning.

When your child has learned the basic "home" words he is ready to move ahead.

By now your child is reading more than fifty words and both you and he should be delighted. Two points should be made before continuing to the next step, which is the beginning of the end in the process of learning to read.

If the parent has approached teaching his or her child to read as sheer pleasure (as should ideally be the case) rather than as a duty or obligation (which in the end is not a good enough reason), then both the parent and child should be enjoying themselves immensely in the daily sessions.

John Ciardi, in the editorial already mentioned, said of the child, "... if he has been loved (which is basically to say, if he has been played with by parents who found honest pleasure in the play)... " This is a superb description of love—play *and* learning with a child—and it should never be far from a parent's mind while teaching a child to read.

The next point for a parent to remember is that children are vastly curious about words, whether written or spoken. When a child expresses interest in a word, for whatever reason, it is now wise to print it for him and add it to his vocabulary. He will learn very quickly and easily any word that he has asked about.

Therefore, if a child should ask, "Mommy, what is a rhinoceros?" or "What does microscopic mean?" it is very wise to answer the question carefully and then print the word immediately, and so add it to his reading vocabulary.

He will feel a special pride and get additional pleasure from learning to read words that he himself generated.

THE SECOND STEP—*Couplets*

Once a child has acquired a basic reading vocabulary of single words he is now ready to put those words together to make couplets (two-word combinations).

This is an important intermediate step between single words and whole sentences. Couplets create a bridge between the basic building blocks of reading—single words—and the next unit of organization—the sentence. Of course the ability to read a whole group of related words, called a sentence, is the next large objective. However, this intermediate step of couplets will help the child to progress by easy steps to this next level.

Now Mother reviews her child's vocabulary and determines what couplets she can make using the words she has already taught. She will quickly discover that she needs some modifying words in her child's vocabulary diet in order to be able to make couplets that make sense.

One simple group of words that are very helpful and easy to teach are basic colors:

Colors

red	violet	blue
orange	black	pink
yellow	white	gray
green	brown	purple

These words can be made with squares of the appropriate color on the back of each card. Mother can then teach the reading word and flip the card over to reveal the color itself.

Very young children learn colors quickly and easily and take great delight in pointing out colors wherever they go. After the basic colors have been taught there is a whole world of more subtle shades to be explored (indigo, azure, chartreuse, olive, gold, silver, copper, etc.).

Once these simple colors have been introduced, Mother can make her child's first set of couplets:

orange juice	pink toes
blue eyes	violet grapes
red truck	brown hair
yellow banana	green apple
black shoe	white refrigerator

Each of these couplets has the great virtue that the child knows both words as single words. The couplet contains two basic elements that are satisfying to the child. One aspect he enjoys is seeing old words he already knows. The second element is that although he already knows these two words he now sees that his two old words combined create a new idea. This is exciting to him. It opens the door on understanding the magic of the printed page.

Divide the couplets you have created into two sets of five couplets each. Show each set three times a day for five days (or less). After five days, retire one couplet from each set and add one new couplet to each set. Continue to add one new couplet to each set and retire an old one daily.

As Mother progresses with this step she will feel the need of additional modifiers. These will best be taught in pairs as opposites:

Opposites

big	little	long	short
fat	thin	right	left
clean	dirty	happy	sad
smooth	rough	empty	full
pretty	ugly	dark	light

Again, depending on the age and experience of the child you may or may not need to introduce these cards with a picture on the back of the card to illustrate the idea. "Big" and "little" are very simple ideas for a very young child. What little child does not instantly recognize when his older brother or sister has been given something "bigger" than he has received? We adults are apt to view these ideas as abstractions and they are, but these ideas surround the young child and he grasps them very quickly when they are presented in a logical and straightforward manner. These ideas are very closely related to his day-to-day survival so they are, in a manner of speaking, close to his heart.

We can now present:

Couplets

empty cup	full cup
big chair	little chair
happy Mommy	sad Mommy
long hair	short hair
clean shirt	dirty shirt
right hand	left hand

THE THIRD STEP—*Phrases*

It is a simple step to hop from couplets to phrases. When we do, the leap is made by adding action to the couplets and creating a very basic short sentence.

> **Mommy is jumping.**

> **Billy is reading.**

> **Daddy is eating.**

Even with a basic vocabulary of fifty to seventy-five words the possible combinations are many. There are three excellent ways to teach simple phrases and a wise mother will use not one, but all three.

1. Using the single reading cards you have already made, make some "is" cards. Sit down with five names of people or animals, five "is" cards, and five "actions." Choose one of each and put together a phrase. Read it to your child. Now let your child choose one of each group and make a phrase. Read his phrase to him. Together make three to five phrases. Then put the cards away. You can play this game as often

as your child likes. Remember to change the nouns and verbs often to keep the game fresh.

Mommy	is	eating
Daddy	is	sleeping
Sally	is	laughing
Jimmy	is	running
Amy	is	climbing

Mother's choice

| Sally | is | climbing |

Child's choice

| Jimmy | is | running |

2. Using your (approximately) 6" x 22" posterboard cards make a set of five phrases. You will have to decrease your print size in order to fit three or four words on to the cards. Now make your letters 2" high rather than 3". As you do

this be sure not to crowd the words. Leave enough white space so each word can "breathe." Show them three times daily for five days (or less). Then add two *new* phrases daily and retire two old ones daily. Your child will learn these very quickly, so be willing to move on to new phrases as quickly as possible.

The elephant is eating

3. Make a simple phrase book. This book should have five phrases with a simple illustration for each phrase. Again, use common sense in choosing the size of the pages. If your sheets of posterboard are 22" x 28", simply cut them into quarters to make pages that are 11" x 14" with 2" red lettering. The printed page precedes and is separated from the illustration. It is wise to make the first such book a simple diary of your child's day.

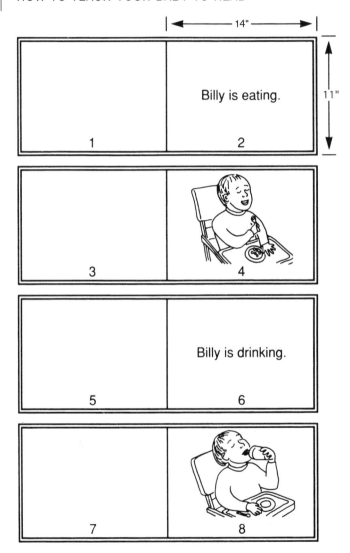

His new book can easily be illustrated using photographs of your child doing each of these things. This little book becomes the first in a long series of books that trace the growth and development and the life and times of your child. These books are naturally loved by every child lucky enough to have a mother who takes the time to make them. Each book starts out as a modest little ten-page book that Mother reads to her child two to three times daily for a few days. Then Mother introduces a new chapter that uses the same basic vocabulary.

These wonderful little homemade diaries of your child's life are a living, breathing way to use all the great photographs that every mother has taken of her child over the years.

THE FOURTH STEP—*Sentences*

In truth the simple phrases we have just discussed are also short sentences. But now the child is ready for the most important step after being able to differentiate single words. Now he is ready to tackle full sentences that express a more complete thought.

If we could understand only sentences that we had seen and known before, our reading would indeed be limited. All of the anticipation in opening a new book lies in finding what the book is going to say that we have never read before.

To recognize individual words and to realize that they represent an object or an idea is a basic step in learning to read. To recognize that words, when used in a sentence, can represent a more complicated idea is an additional and vitally important step.

We now can use the same basic procedures introduced when we began phrases. However we now go beyond three words. Instead of choosing from five nouns and five verbs to make the simple phrase "Mommy is eating," now we add five objects and present "Mommy is eating a banana."

Again we need a group of "a," "an," or "the" cards. These do not need to be taught separately as the child will learn them in the context of the sentence where they serve a purpose and make sense; outside the context they are of little interest to the child.

While he uses the word "the" correctly in ordinary speech and therefore understands it, he does not deal with it as an isolated word. It is, of course, vital to reading that he *recognize* and *read* it as a separate word, but it is not necessary that he be able to define it. In the same way, all children speak correctly long before they know the rules of grammar. Besides, how would you like to explain what "the" means, even to a ten-year-old? So don't. Just be sure he can read it.

When you have made four-word sentences using the three methods described in the third step (phrases), then you can add modifiers—adjectives and adverbs—that give life to a proper sentence:

Mommy is eating a yellow banana.

Again, as you add additional words you will need to decrease the print size a little bit. Now decrease the size of your letters to about 1 ½". Give each word plenty of room on the page.

If you have been playing the game of making sentences with your child consistently you will already have noticed that your child delights in making sentences that are ridiculous or absurd.

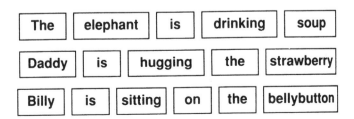

This should inspire you to do the same. It is a sad commentary that our formal education was so drab and sterile that without realizing it we avoid using humor and absurdity in our teaching. We were so often reminded not to "be silly" or "act ridiculous" that we assume it is against the law to have fun when one is teaching or learning. This notion is the very soul of absurdity for fun *is* learning and learning *is* fun. *The more fun going on, the more learning is taking place.*

A good sentence-making session usually finds mother and child trying to outdo each other in creating riotous combinations and ends with a lot of noisy tickling, hugging, and merriment.

Since every sentence you are creating or putting on cards or in books is composed of single words that you have already carefully taught beforehand, it is probable that your child will go through many sentences very quickly.

You are wise to take a limited vocabulary of perhaps fifty words and use them to make as many sentences as you and your child can create. In this way your child will really strengthen his mastery of these words. His confidence will grow so that no matter what combination or permutation is presented in a new sentence he will be able to decode it.

At this stage you are still presenting this

material to him. You are reading the sentences or books aloud to him. Depending on his age, language ability, or personality, he may be actually saying some words aloud spontaneously or reading whole sentences aloud. If he does this spontaneously that is fine. However you should not ask him to read aloud to you. We will discuss this point at length later in the next chapter.

As you go from four-word sentences to five-word sentences and longer, you will no doubt begin to run out of space on the 6" x 22" cards or the 11" x 14" books.

Now by *evolution* you are going to do three things:

1. Reduce the print size.
2. Increase the number of words.
3. Change the print from red to black.

Begin by reducing print size a little bit. You do not want to reduce it so much that your child has the slightest difficulty with it. Try 1" print. Use this for several weeks. If this does not appear to be a problem then you are ready to increase the number of words. If you have been using five-word sentences now go to six-word sentences. However leave the print size at 1". Now continue with six-word sentences for awhile. If all goes well, then reduce your print size to approximately ⅞". *The important rule to observe in this process is never to reduce print size and increase the number of words at the same time.* First reduce print size slightly and live with it for awhile, then increase the number of words.

Do both of these things gradually. Remember, the sentence cannot be too big or too clear, but it could be too small or too confusing. You never want to rush this process.

If you did reduce the print size too quickly or increased the number of words too fast, you will notice your child's attention and interest dropping. He might begin to look away from the printed matter altogether and simply look at you because the card or page is visually too complex for him. If this should occur, simply return to the print size or number of words you were using *right before* this happened and his enthusiasm will return. Stay at this level for a good while longer before attempting to change things again.

You do not really need to change the size or color of single words. In fact we have found that keeping single words large is easier for both mother and child.

However, when you are making books with one-inch letters or six words on a page or longer, we recommend changing from red to black print. As words get smaller, black does provide better contrast and a more legible page.

Now the stage has been set for the final and most exciting step of all—the book. We have already gotten our foot solidly in the door by creating many little couplet books, phrase books, and sentence books, but if these steps are the skeleton, it is the next one that is the meat.

The path has been cleared, so let's get to it.

THE FIFTH STEP—*Books*

Now your child is ready to read a real and proper book. The fact is he has already read many homemade books and completed all the single words, couplets, and phrases that he will find in his first book.

The careful preparation that has gone before is the key to his success in his first book and indeed for many books to come.

His ability to handle very large-print single words, couplets, phrases, and sentences has been established. But now he must be able to handle smaller print and a greater number of words on each page.

The younger a child is, the more challenging

this step will be. Remember that as you have taught him to read, you have actually been growing his visual pathway exactly as exercise grows the biceps.

In the event you are reducing the print size too quickly and therefore presenting print that your child is not yet capable of reading easily, you will have a clear indication of what print size *is* easy and comfortable for your child from doing the *third* and *fourth steps* of your program.

Since the words he is using are exactly the same words but differ only in the fact that they become smaller with each step, you can now see quite clearly if a child is learning faster than his visual pathway is able to mature.

As an example, suppose that a child completes the *third* and *fourth steps* successfully with 2" words but has difficulty in reading the identical words in the book itself. The answer is simple. The words are too small. We know that the child can read 2" words easily. Now the parent simply prepares additional words and simple sentences 2" in height. Use simple, imaginative words and sentences that the child will enjoy reading. After two months of this, return again to the book with its smaller print.

Remember that if the print were made too small *you* would also have trouble reading it.

If the child is three years of age by the time

you get to the ⅞" print of the book itself, you will probably not be held up at all at this point. If the child is less than two years old by the time you get to the book, it is almost certain that you will need to obtain or create additional books with 1" or 2" print for the child. Fine, it is all reading, and real reading at that. It will mature his brain growth far more than would otherwise be the case.

The parent will now need to procure the book which he will teach his child to read. Find a book that contains vocabulary that you have already taught as single words, couplets, and phrases. The choice of the book to be used is very important; it should meet the following standards:

1. It should have a vocabulary of fifty to one hundred words.
2. It should present no more than one sentence on a single page.
3. The printing should be no less than ⅞" high.
4. Text should precede and be separated from illustrations.

Unfortunately, at present, few commercial books meet all of these requirements. Examples of books published by The Gentle Revolution

Press with these requirements in mind are:

1. *Enough, Inigo, Enough*
2. *Nose Is Not Toes*

However, one or two books will hardly be enough to keep your eager young reader fed and happy—you will need *many*. Therefore, the simplest means of providing your child with proper books at this stage is to buy interesting and well-written commercial books and make them over with the large, clear printed pages your young child requires. You can then cut out the professional illustrations and include them in the book you are making.

Sometimes it will be necessary to simplify the text to suit your child's reading. Or you may find books with beautiful illustrations but silly or repetitive text that would bore your child. In this case rewrite the text using more sophisticated vocabulary and more mature sentence structure.

The content of the book is vital. Your child will want to read a book for the exact same reasons that we adults read books. He will expect to be entertained or given new information —preferably both. He will enjoy well-written adventure stories, fairy tales, and mysteries. There is a world of wonderful fiction already written and waiting to be written. He will also enjoy nonfiction. Books that teach him about the lives of famous people or animals are vastly popular with tiny children.

Perhaps the easiest rule to follow is, do you find the book interesting? If not, the chances are excellent your three-year-old won't find much to interest him either.

It is far, far better to aim a bit over his head and let him reach upward than to run the risk of boring him with pap and pablum.

Remember the following rules:

1. Create or choose books that will be interesting to your child.
2. Introduce all new vocabulary as single words before beginning the book.
3. Make the text large and clear.
4. Make sure your child has to turn the page to see the illustration that follows the text.

Once you have completed the above steps, you are ready to begin the book with your child.

Sit down with him and read the book to him. He may want to read some of the words instead of having you do it. If he does this spontaneously, fine. This will depend largely on his age and personality. The younger a child is, the less he will wish to read aloud. In this case you read and he will follow along.

Read at a natural speed, with enthusiasm and a lot of expression in your voice. It is not necessary to point to each word as you read. However, your child may wish to do so. If he does, this is fine, as long as you do not slow down.

Read the book two to three times daily for several days. Each book will have its own life. Some books are ready for the shelf in a few days, others are demanded daily for weeks.

Your child now begins his own library of books. Once you have retired a book, it goes on his shelf. He may then read it himself as many times a day as he likes.

As this little library of superb custom-made books grows, it is the source of much pleasure and pride to the tiny child. At this stage he will probably begin taking one of his books with him wherever he goes.

While other children are bored driving in the car, waiting in line at the supermarket, or sitting in a restaurant, your little fellow has his books—his old books, which he cherishes and reads again and again, and his new books, which he looks forward to every week.

At this point it is impossible to provide too many books. He will devour them. The more he gets the more he wants. In a world where 30 to 45 percent of the eighteen-year-olds in our school system are not able to read at grade level, this problem of keeping the young child supplied with books is the right problem to have.

SUMMARY

There are three distinct levels of understanding in the process of learning how to read. As the child conquers each of them he will show exuberance at his new and very exciting discovery. The joy Columbus must have known in finding a new world could hardly have been greater than that which the child will experience at each of these levels.

Naturally, his first pleasure and delight is in the disclosure that words have meaning. To the child this is almost like a secret code that he shares with grownups. He will enjoy this vastly and visibly.

Next he notices that the words he reads can be used together and are therefore more than merely labels for objects. This is also a new and wonderful revelation.

The last discovery he makes will probably be

very noticeable to the parent. This, the greatest of them all, is that the book he is reading represents more than the simple fun of translating secret names into objects, and more even than the decoding of strings of words into comments about objects and people. Suddenly and delightfully the big secret bursts upon the child that this book is actually talking to him, and to him alone. When the child comes to this realization (and this does not necessarily happen until he has read many books), there will be no stopping him. He will now be a reader in every sense of the word. He now realizes that the words he already knows can be rearranged to make entirely new ideas. He does not have to learn a new set of words every time he has to read something.

What a discovery this is! Few things will compare to it in later life. He can now have an adult talking to him in a new conversation any time he wants, simply by picking up a new book.

All of man's knowledge is now available to him. Not only the knowledge of people he knows in his home and neighborhood, but people far away whom he will never see. Even more than that, he can be approached by people who lived long ago in other places and in other ages.

The power to control our own fate began, as

we shall see, with our ability to write and to read. Because man has been able to write and to read, he has been able to pass on to future generations centuries later and in remote places the knowledge he has gained. Man's knowledge is cumulative.

Man is man essentially because he can read and write.

This is the true importance of what your child discovers when he learns to read. The child may even try in his own way to tell you about his great discovery, lest you, his parent, miss it. If he does, listen to him respectfully and with love. What he has to say is important.

8
the perfect age
to begin

He can't learn any younger.

—WILLIAM RICKER,
1890

You now understand the basic steps in the reading pathway. These steps apply regardless of the age of your child. However, how you actually begin with your child and which steps may need to be emphasized depends upon the age of your child when you begin your reading program.

The pathway we have just described is the pathway to follow and it works. Tens of thousands of parents have used this precise method to teach children at every age between birth and six to read successfully. However, it is to be remembered that a newborn is in no way the same person as a two-year-old. A three-month-old is certainly not the same as a three-year-old.

We are now able to refine that program to design individual programs for each important age group from birth to six.

The steps of the pathway do not change regardless of age. The sequence of the steps of the pathway remain the same regardless of age.

In this chapter we will outline the refinements and nuances that will enhance your reading program and enable you to succeed more easily no matter what age your baby may be when you begin your program.

At this point there may be a temptation to read and study only the section that pertains to your child at this moment. However, it is important to understand all of the points covered in each section so that as your child grows and develops you understand how to change and reshape his program.

Your child will be changing constantly and your program must be dynamic and ever-changing to keep pace with him.

THE NEWBORN CHILD

It is important to know if you intend to start at birth, that at first your program is not a reading program—it is really a program of visual stimulation.

In the context of our Reading Pathway the newborn child needs the step *before* the *first step*. We shall call this the *zero step* because before he can truly be ready for the *first step* of his reading program he needs the *zero step,* which is a program of visual stimulation.

At birth your baby can see only light and dark. He cannot yet see detail. Within the first few hours or days of life he will begin to see outlines poorly for brief periods. As his ability to see outlines is stimulated by opportunities to see outlines all around him, he will begin for *very* brief periods to see detail poorly. By very brief periods we mean a few seconds. At this stage, seeing outline is an effort for a newborn. Seeing detail is a monumental effort. However, it is an effort he is willing to make because his need to see is so strong.

Newborns begin to see the dark shape of Mother's head moving in front of the light of a sunny window. The more opportunity the infant has to see this contrast of a stable black outline on a well-lighted background the better his vision becomes.

Once he can see outline, he begins to search for detail within the outline. Mother's eyes, nose, or mouth are the details he sees first.

It is not within the scope of this book to describe in detail the growth and development of the visual pathway of the newborn baby. However, showing a tiny infant reading words does play an important part in stimulating and developing the ability to see detail.

*This ability is a result of stimulation and opportunity. It is **not** a matter of some preset hereditary alarm clock ringing and causing it to happen, as has been previously believed.*

The newborn who is presented with opportunity to see outline and detail will develop these abilities more quickly and thus will graduate more quickly from being functionally blind, as he is at birth, to being able to see well without effort.

This visual stimulation program is extremely easy and, when you think about it, totally logical. After all, you are talking to your baby at birth. Indeed, have you not been talking to him for the nine months prior to his delivery?

No one would question the sense of talking to a newborn baby. We all recognize that it is the birthright of every baby to hear his language.

And yet spoken language is a wild abstraction. We could say it is no more or less abstract than written language, but the truth is that spoken language is actually a good bit harder for the tiny baby to decode than written language. It is a basic tenet of all teaching to be consistent. And yet it is very difficult when using spoken language to be consistent. We are apt to say to the tiny infant, "How are *you?*" Later we may say, "*How* are you?" And before the day ends, "How *are* you?"

We have said the same thing three times. But is it the same thing?

To the immature auditory pathway of the tiny infant these are three different things; each one has a different emphasis. He is looking for the similarities and the differences between these three questions.

Now consider the advantages of the visual pathway. We take our large white card with large red print that says "Mommy." We hold it up and say "Mommy." We show this card many times throughout the day. To the tiny infant, each time he sees the card it looks identical to the card he has seen before. Indeed, it looks the same because it *is* the same. The result is that he learns this much more quickly and easily through his visual pathway than he would have through his auditory pathway.

You should begin with single words. Choose seven words that are the words you use most often and are therefore most needed by your newborn–his own name, the words *Mommy* and *Daddy,* plus the parts of his body. These are a good way to begin.

Since you are beginning with a newborn, your first set of words needs to be *very* large. Use posterboard that is 6" by 22". Your lettering should be 5" tall and ¾" thick or thicker. You need very *bold* lettering to get the appropriate intensity for an infant. Remember, this is visual stimulation, first and foremost.

If you are starting at birth, or shortly there-after, you will want to begin with one word. Usually your child's name is a fine place to start. While you are cradling your baby in your arms hold up the card about eighteen inches from him and say his name. Now hold the card and wait. You will watch him do his best to lo-cate the card. When he does see it, say the word again loudly and clearly. He will try to focus for a second or two–now put the card away.

Because a tiny infant cannot see outline or detail, there is a temptation to sweep visual in-formation across his field of vision in an attempt to catch his attention.

Remember, he has superb attention but very poor vision. If we sweep the word in front of him, he must attempt to focus on a moving object. This is much more difficult than locating a stationary object. Therefore, you should hold the card absolutely still and give him the time he needs to locate the card. At first it will take ten to fifteen seconds, or even longer, but each day you will observe a measurable decrease in the time it takes him to locate the card and focus on it briefly.

His ability to locate the card and focus on it will be a product of how many times we show him the word. Each time it will be a little bit easier than the time before.

It is extremely important to provide excellent lighting. The light should be directed toward the card, never in the eyes of the baby. This lighting needs to be markedly better than what is considered adequate ambient light for you and me.

You will be accelerating and enhancing the incredible process of the development of human vision from the crude ability to see light to the more sophisticated ability to recognize Mother's smile from across the room.

On the first day show one word. Show this word ten times that day. If you can show it even more often, that is very good. Many mothers keep their reading cards where they diaper their babies. Each time the baby is changed,

Mother takes the opportunity to show him his word. This works very well.

The second day choose a second word and show that ten times. Each day for seven days choose a different word and show it ten times in the day. At the beginning of the following week go back to the word with which you started and again show it ten times. Repeat this process for three weeks. This will mean, for example, that every Monday the baby will see *Mommy* ten times.

By now, if you started at birth, your three-week-old baby is definitely able to focus on his words more quickly. In fact, as soon as you pull out a word, he may immediately show signs of excitement and anticipation by wiggling his body and kicking his legs.

When this happens, it is a most exciting moment for you because you now realize that your baby is not only seeing but is understanding what he sees, and, even more important, he is enjoying the experience tremendously. Each day this program of visual stimulation becomes easier and easier for your baby as his ability to focus and see detail develops.

In the early stages of visual development you will find that your tiny infant's visual ability varies throughout the day. When he is well rested and fed, he will be using his visual abilities constantly but will tire very quickly. When he is sleepy, he will turn off his vision and see very little. When he is hungry, he will put his energy into convincing you to feed him.

Therefore, you must choose the correct time to show him a word. You will quickly learn to anticipate his best times and avoid the hungry or sleepy times. Sometimes he may be under the weather for a day or two. This may make him cranky and out of sorts almost all the time. Don't show him words on these days–wait until he is back to his old self.

Then start back exactly where you left off. You do not need to go back and review.

After the first seven words have been repeated for three weeks choose seven new words and cycle through them in the same way until your tiny infant is seeing detail consistently and easily. In the average baby who is receiving no organized stimulation, this will not happen until twelve weeks or later. In your baby who has had a program of visual stimulation, this may occur between eight to ten weeks.

Mothers are superb at knowing when their infants can see them easily. At this point a tiny baby recognizes Mother easily and instantly responds to her smile without needing any auditory or tactile clues. At this point a baby is using his vision almost all the time. It is only during the rare moment of extreme fatigue or illness when he turns off his vision.

You have now fully completed the *zero step* with your baby and he is ready to graduate to the *first step* because you have actually grown his visual pathway. He is ready to begin on the Reading Pathway and to follow the program outlined there (Chapter 7). Since your baby has already been seeing single words for one or two months, you can move right into three groups of five words three times daily.

At this point your program shifts gears from the slow and deliberate visual stimulation program to a very fast-paced reading program. Now your baby will take in reading words at an astounding rate, just as he is learning language through his ear at an astounding rate.

STARTING WITH AN INFANT
(Three Months to Six Months)

If you are beginning your reading program with a three- to six-month-old, he will be *majoring* in the *first step* of the Reading Pathway. This step will be the heart of your program.

The two most important things to remember are:

1. Show words very quickly.
2. Add new words often.

The wonderful thing about a tiny infant is that he is a pure intellectual. He learns anything with a total impartiality and without any bias whatsoever. He learns for learning's sake, without any strings attached. Of course, his survival depends on this characteristic but it is an admirable characteristic and is no less admirable for being tied to his survival.

He is the kind of intellectual we would all like to be but very few of us are. He loves everything there is to learn. It is his glory *and* ours if we are lucky enough to get the opportunity to teach him.

Between three months and six months of age a tiny baby is able to take in language at an astounding rate. He is also seeing detail consistently. In short, he is able to absorb spoken language without the slightest difficulty, as long as we make that information *loud* and clear. He is able to absorb written language as long as we make it *large* and clear. It is our objective to keep reading words large and bold so that the baby can always see them easily.

At this stage a baby is using sounds to talk to us. However, it will be months before we are able to decode all these sounds as the words, sentences, and paragraphs that they are. In adult terms, then, the baby cannot talk.

He has superb sensory pathways to take in information, but he has not yet developed the motor pathways sufficiently to get information back out in a way that can readily be understood.

Since this is the case, someone will no doubt ask you how you can teach a baby to read when he cannot yet talk. *Reading is done with the visual pathway, not the mouth.* Reading is the process of taking in language in its written form. Speech is the process of putting out language in its oral form.

Reading is a sensory ability as is hearing. Talking is a motor ability as is writing. Talking and writing require motor skills that the baby doesn't have.

The fact that your child is too young to speak and is not able to say his reading words does not negate the fact that you are increasing and enriching his language by teaching him to read.

Indeed such investments in teaching the baby to read will *speed* his talking and broaden his vocabulary. Remember that language is language, whether transmitted to the brain via the eye or via the ear.

At the Institutes for the Achievement of Human Potential we use reading as one of the important means of teaching brain-injured children to speak.

Reading aloud for a four-month-old is impossible. This is to his great advantage since no one will be tempted to try to get him to do this. He can read as you and I read–silently, quickly, effectively.

At this age a tiny child is truly a glutton for information. He will probably demand more information than you are able to give him. When you begin your reading program you may often find that at the end of a session he will demand more. Resist the temptation of repeating his words again or doing another group just then. He might happily see four or five groups of words and still want more.

You can actually show several sets back-to-back with a three- or four-month-old and get away with it for a few months, but be prepared to change in the near future because you will need to do so.

Remember he is a linguistic genius–be prepared to feed him with a lot of new single words.

STARTING WITH A LITTLE BABY
(Seven to Twelve Months)

If you are beginning with a seven- to twelve-month-old the two most important things to keep in mind are:

1. Keep every session *very* brief.
2. Have sessions often.

As we have said, a four-month-old will sometimes want to see all his sets of words one after the other at one session. However such a procedure would be a disaster for a seven- to eighteen-month-old.

Use only one group of five words at a session and then put them away.

The reason for this is simple. Each day your baby's mobility will be expanding. At three months he is relatively sedentary. He is a watcher. He will watch his words for long periods. We adults love this, so we get into the habit of showing him *all* his words at one sitting. We get used to this routine; it is easy for us. But each day this baby is changing. He is getting more and more mobile. As soon as he is creeping on hands and knees a whole world of new possibilities opens up for him. He now has a driver's license and he is just dying to explore. All of a sudden this sedentary little fellow, who saw fifty words quite happily, is no longer sedentary. He has no time at all for his reading. We become discouraged. Where have we gone wrong? He must not like reading anymore. Baffled, we give up.

The baby must be baffled too. He was having such a good time reading and then the words disappeared. It wasn't that he stopped liking reading, it was that his schedule became busier. He now had an entire household to explore. He has all those kitchen cabinets to open and close, all those plugs to investigate, every piece of fuzz on the carpet has to be picked up and eaten before the sun sets. You have to admit that there is an awful lot on a seven-month-old's plate when it comes to search and destroy. He still wants to explore reading too but he cannot afford fifty words at one time. Five words at one time is far, far better.

If we provide him with brief sessions, he will continue to gobble up new words at a mile a minute. It is only when we make him late to his next pressing appointment by taking more than a few seconds that he is forced to abandon ship and leave us sitting alone in the middle of the living room floor.

We adults love to find a nice comfortable

schedule and then stick to it no matter what. Children are dynamic—they never stop changing. Just as we have established a routine, the tiny child moves on to a new level and we find we must move with him or be left behind.

Because this is so, always keep sessions brief; then as his mobility expands you will be in the habit of brief sessions, which are a natural part of his busy schedule and fit in with his agenda.

STARTING WITH A BABY
(Twelve Months to Eighteen Months)

If you are beginning your reading program with a child of this age the two most important things to remember are:

1. Very, very brief sessions.
2. Stop before he wants to stop.

In terms of the Reading Pathway you will be emphasizing the *first* and *second step* (Chapter 7). As you work your way up the Reading Pathway with a child at this particular stage of development, the most important refinement is to keep the duration of every session *very, very* brief.

The reason this is so important is that now his mobility development becomes extremely important.

At twelve months, a baby is either walking or beginning the process of moving between people or furniture while holding on with his hands in order to work his way by degrees to his first independent steps. By the time that same child is eighteen months he will not only have become a good, steady walker but he will have begun to run. This is quite an accomplishment in six short months. In order to achieve these spectacular results he must put a great deal of time and energy into feats of physical daring.

At no other point in his life will physical movement assume the importance that it does at this moment. You can be assured that if you were to attempt to follow your baby and simply do each of the things he does physically during the day you would be absolutely exhausted after a single hour of his routine. It has been tried.

No adult is physically up to the rigors of what the average twelve- to eighteen-month-old can handle in a given day.

These physical activities are of great importance to the tiny child. During this period of his growth and development we have to be especially wise about adapting his reading program to his intense physical program. Up to this moment in his life a group of five words at one session may be perfect. However, during this stage you may need to drop to three words at a session or two or even one.

There is no single principle of teaching that will take you further than that of always stopping before your child wants to stop.

Always stop before *he* wants to stop.

Always stop *before* he wants to stop.

Always stop before he wants to stop.

This principle is true for all teaching of all human beings at all stages of development and at any age.

But it is *most especially* true for the twelve- to eighteen-month-old.

He needs a high frequency, low duration schedule. Lots of brief sessions suit him. Indeed he needs those brief, treasured respites from his labors.

He will love the entire Reading Pathway from the *first step* of single words to the *fifth step* of books but he will *major* in the *first* and *second steps* because he is a man on the move and cannot afford to tarry for very long.

Very short and sweet sessions are best for him.

STARTING WITH A LITTLE CHILD
(Eighteen Months to Thirty Months)

Beginning *anything* new or different with an eighteen- to thirty-month-old can be a challenge. He is, of course, highly capable and will move through the *first step* to the *fifth step* rapidly *once* we have a happy consistent program started. There are three important points to remember when you are teaching this little fellow:

1. Choose the words *he* likes best.
2. Start his reading program *gradually.*
3. Move from single words and couplets to *phrases* as quickly as possible.

As each day passes he develops and he assumes his own viewpoint. He begins to have his own likes and dislikes. The eighteen-month-old is not the pure intellectual he was at three months.

If we are going to begin to introduce language in visual form to an eighteen-month-old, we first must remember that he is already an expert at language auditorally. Although he has been talking for months, it is only now that the adults around him can understand his sounds as words. It is not surprising that when he realizes he is at last being understood he has a lot to say and a number of demands to make.

It is important to keep in mind that if an idea is *his* idea it's a great idea; if an idea originates elsewhere it may not have his approval.

No one occupies center stage quite as completely and confidently as this fellow. This is his glory and his program needs to be designed with this in mind.

Look around at his environment. Observe what are the things he adores. These are the things that he will want to see as reading words. He is well beyond being interested in his toes or his fingers. He will want his vocabulary to reflect a wider sphere of belongings–foods, actions, even emotions. You can teach adjectives and adverbs to this fellow. So the first thing to remember is to *choose words carefully*. Find the words he wants. Throw away the ones he doesn't like.

The second thing to remember is that you cannot go from no reading program to a full-blown reading program in a single day with this little guy.

Instead of beginning on the first day with three sets of five words as outlined in Chapter 7, begin with only one group of five words. This will pique his interest without going overboard. You need to woo him a little.

He will love his words once he decides it is *his idea* and they are *his words,* but at first they are your words and he doesn't know them.

Show him that one group of five words very quickly and then put them away. Come back at another good moment later. In a few days add another group of five words and so by *evolution* as his interest grows, introduce new groups of five words as the days go on.

It is best to starve him a little and have him pressuring you for more. As you get into your program, ask him what words he would like and make those words for him.

As soon as you have retired enough single words and couplets to make some funny phrases, do so. He will love phrases, so don't wait until you have done thousands of single words to get to phrases. He is not a baby. He will want phrases more than single words, so get to them as quickly as you can.

He will be delighted to major in the *third step* on the Reading Pathway and beyond as long as we choose each word we use in the *first step* and each couplet we use in the *second step* to his specifications and we begin that very *first step* by evolution rather than revolution.

A word about your eighteen- to thirty-month-old saying the words aloud. A child of two, as everyone knows, does exactly and precisely what pleases him most. If he wishes to shout out his reading words, he may do so. If he doesn't wish to say them, he won't. The point is to teach your child whatever his age may be and recognize his right to demonstrate his knowledge in the way *he* chooses—or—not at all.

STARTING WITH A YOUNG CHILD
(Thirty Months to Forty-eight Months)

A child of this age and older wants to get to the final step of the Reading Pathway (the *fifth step*) instantly.

However he will need to follow that pathway from the *first step* in order to major in his favorite—the *fifth step*. He will want books, and the sooner the better, but he will require a bit more time to learn single words than a baby requires.

The three most important things to remember are:

1. He will need sophisticated reading words.
2. He will not learn single words as quickly as a baby.
3. He will want books, books, and more books.

At thirty months your child is certainly no longer a baby. Your baby is now a full-fledged little girl or little boy.

Your child at this stage will not insist on occupying center stage at every instant as he did a year ago. However, his personality is even more established now and so are his likes and dislikes.

He must help you to design his program. If you realize this, the reading program will go very well from the start. Instead of using parts of the body, begin from his area of greatest interest and enthusiasm. If your child loves cars then start by teaching car words. It may not seem the most sensible way to begin to you and me, but it *is* because it means we are beginning with the part of your child's language that interests him most. He has all the time in the world to learn all those mundane words like *cat* and *hat*. He will want words he can get his teeth around. Don't bother him with parts of the body unless you mean *skull, collarbone,* and *humerus.* These will intrigue him because they will *expand* his knowledge of language.

Remember he is not a baby. He will not learn single words nearly as quickly as a baby does. You will need to come back to retired words and use them again and again in books to make him a confident reader.

Nor does it mean you can move like molasses with him. He still will learn at an amazing rate. It just won't equal a baby's rate of learning.

You will need to get into couplets, phrases, and books much more quickly with him than with a younger child. Again, the younger child takes in raw facts more easily and retains information more readily with less reinforcement. Couplets, phrases, and books are the ideal way to cover old vocabulary in a new way that is fun and very useful to the thirty- to forty-eight-month-old child.

Even after one showing, a child of this age is apt to feel he knows a word simply because he realizes he has seen it before. However he will actually need a bit more exposure to that word before he really owns it.

You can keep coming back to show him words he has seen before only if at the same time you keep to your schedule of adding new words. If he knows there will always be new words every day, he will be happy about seeing yesterday's words and even the words from the day before.

Again the real key with him is to get to couplets, phrases, and books quickly. This will make all the difference in the world to him. If you simply stay with single words all the time, you will lose him. He needs to *use* his single words as soon as possible.

He loves the *fifth step* but he needs lots of the *third* and *fourth steps* to insure that the *first* and *second* steps get all the reinforcement they need.

STARTING WITH A CHILD
(Forty-eight Months to Seventy-two Months)

Everything that is important for a thirty- to forty-eight-month-old is even more true for a child between the ages of forty-eight months and seventy-two months of age.

Let's summarize those points:

1. He will not take in raw facts (single words) as quickly as a baby.
2. He will not retain raw facts as easily as a baby.

3. He will have *very* strongly developed likes and dislikes.
4. He will need couplets, phrases, and books to be introduced quickly to reinforce the single words that have been retired.
5. He should be the designer of his reading program by choosing the vocabulary he likes and wants to learn.

At this point mothers are apt to look at their four-year-olds a bit wistfully and say, "Well kid, I guess you're over the hill."

Not so.

Yes, compared to a six-month-old, a two-year-old *is* over the hill but what of that? A four-year-old is an absolute fire-eater compared to an eight-year-old or even a six-year-old, so let's stop worrying and get on with it. There are thousands of superb readers who started when they were four.

Your four-year-old has a real treat in store for him and there isn't a moment to lose. Again, start from your child's interests. If he is a tool maniac, go down in the basement and get out all the tools and find out what they are. Start by making single words of every tool in the house. Get yourself a thesaurus and look up synonyms.

Then you can take the word *fat* and make a set of words that mean fat—elephantine, portly, stout, obese, or rotund. These will go a long way with your child.

There are more than a half million words in the English language. You will have no difficulty in finding hundreds and hundreds of words that your child finds fascinating.

Again, don't lose any sleep over *cat* and *hat*. Start with sophisticated words and stay with sophisticated words. Once your child gets into his reading program he will pick up everyday words on his own without difficulty. It will be very easy to come back to the everyday vocabulary and teach it once you have your foot in the door. The point is you must begin in *his* territory to get his agreement to play the reading game and that is fair enough.

After you have enough single words to write a book, write one. Don't wait until you have done hundreds of single words. After thirty or forty words, start making books immediately using the words you have brought out of retirement.

Your child will want to read books, so make him books based on his single words. You may need to make dozens and dozens of homemade books with large print. This will be a very small investment of time and energy to make, considering his joy in devouring his first books.

We know many wonderful children who were happily reading their way through the fourth-grade section of their local libraries by the time they were six years old, who did not begin to learn to read until they were "over the hill" at four.

At this stage there is an almost overwhelming temptation to ask your child to read aloud.

Reading aloud is an exercise that elementary school children are asked to perform in order to prove they can read.

In fact, reading aloud slows down even a good reader. Whenever the speed of reading drops so does comprehension of what is being read. When comprehension decreases, enjoyment also begins to drop. If we ask the average adult to read the front page of the morning newspaper aloud, when he has finished he will find himself rereading it to find out what the articles were all about.

Reading aloud is not much fun for you and me. It is a *very* poor idea for elementary school children who are struggling to learn to read at six and seven when it is much more difficult to gain this ability than it would have been for them as tiny children.

Even for the older child, asking him to read aloud slows down his reading tremendously. *Remember, when the speed of reading is decreased, comprehension also drops dramatically.* Therefore anything that compromises speed also jeopardizes understanding. Children who learn to read early are very often natural speed readers.

Again the point here is a very simple one: reading is done with the eye and the visual pathway, not with the mouth and the speech pathway. If your child wants to read to you, fine. If he does not, let him read silently; he will read faster and better that way.

We have now covered the basic elements of good teaching, the pathway to follow to teach your child to read, and how to begin with each child.

Testing

We have said much about teaching but absolutely nothing about testing.

Our strongest advice on this subject is do *not* test your child. Babies love to learn but they hate to be tested. In that way they are very like grown-ups. Testing is the opposite of learning. It is full of stress.

To teach a child is to give him a delightful gift.

To test him is to demand payment in advance.

The more you test him, the slower he will learn and the less he will want to.

The less you test him, the quicker he will learn and the more he will want to learn.

Knowledge is the most precious gift you can give your child. Give it as generously as you give him food.

What Is a Test?

What is a test? In essence it is an attempt to find out what the child *doesn't* know. It is putting him on the spot by holding up a card and saying, "What's this say?" or "Can you read this page out loud for your father?" It is essentially disrespectful of the child because he gets the notion that we do not believe he can read unless he proves it–over and over again.

The intention of the test is a negative one–it is to expose what the child does not know.

Winston Churchill once wrote in describing his own experience with school:

"These examinations were a great trial to me. The subjects which were dearest to the examiners were almost invariably those I fancied least...I should have liked to be asked to say what I knew. They always tried to ask what I did not know. When I would have willingly displayed my knowledge, they sought to expose my ignorance. This sort of treatment had only one result: I did not do well in examinations..."

As we have already said and cannot say often enough, the result of testing is to decrease learning and the *willingness* to learn.

Do not test your child and do not allow anyone else to do so either.

Problem-solving Opportunities

Well what is a mother to do? She does not want to test her child, she wants to teach him and give him every opportunity to experience the joy of learning and accomplishment.

Therefore, instead of testing her child she provides problem-solving opportunities.

The purpose of a problem-solving opportunity is for the child to be able to demonstrate what he knows if he wishes to do so.

It is the exact *opposite* of the test. A very simple problem-solving opportunity would be to hold up two of his favorite cards. Let's say you choose "apple" and "banana" and you hold them up and ask, "Where is banana?" This is a good opportunity for a baby to look at or touch the card if he wishes to do so. If your baby looks at the card *banana* or touches it, you are naturally delighted and make a great fuss. If he looks at the other word simply say, "This is *apple*" and *"This* is *banana."* You're happy, enthusiastic, and relaxed. If he does not respond to your question hold the word *banana* a little closer to him and say "This is *banana,* isn't it?" again in a happy, enthusiastic, relaxed way. End of opportunity. *No matter how he responds he wins,* and so do you, because the chances are very good that if you are happy and relaxed he will enjoy doing this with you.

With your two-year-old you might hold up the same two cards but the question would be different: "What did you have on your cornflakes this morning?"

The same problem-solving opportunity for your three-year-old might be: "What is long and yellow and tastes sweet?"

With your four-year-old you might ask, "Which one grows in Brazil?" and with your five-year-old, "Which one contains more potassium?"

The same two simple single words but five very different questions geared to the knowledge and interest of the child.

A properly asked question creates an irresistible problem-solving opportunity.

It is a world away from the dull and tedious world of "What does this say?"

An example would be Reading Card Bingo. Mother chooses a group of 15-30 retired single words like foods or animals or opposites. She then makes a bingo game card for each family member but instead of a grid with numbers she makes her grids very large with large red reading words. A beginner's bingo would have perhaps nine words on a bingo card. Each bingo card has slightly different words so that no two cards are identical. Mother then gives each family member nine chips and instructs them to place a chip on a word on their card if it is called out.

Mother proceeds to call out words, making sure that each child is getting his fair share and helping any child who may have overlooked a word. Whoever fills his card with chips first says, "Bingo!" This game can be played in reverse with, for example, animal pictures on the cards and Mother holding up single reading words of the animal names. As a child moves up the reading pathway the same animal bingo can be played using couplets instead of single words, and then phrases or sentences.

There are so many wonderful games our mothers have created to provide delightful opportunities for their children to use their knowledge in a joyful way. You name it and some clever mother and child have done it and enjoyed every minute of it, too.

These opportunity sessions are an elegant way for your child to demonstrate his success in reading and for you to share in his great accomplishment. If both you and your child thoroughly enjoy these opportunities then they can be used but should never be abused. Don't overdo it, no matter how much fun it is.

If you want to hold up two words and give your child a choice, do not do this more than once a week. Keep the sessions very brief. Do no more than one problem-solving opportunity at a time.

Some children love to choose words and delight in this as long as we don't overdo it. Some children have no interest in choosing words. They will do their best to discourage this by not responding at all or by consistently choosing the opposite word. In either case the message is clear–knock it off.

If for any reason you or your child do not enjoy problem solving, don't do it.

These opportunities for feedback are actually more for you than your child. Your child will be most interested in learning new words and not going back over old words he already knows.

SUMMARY

Once you have begun to teach your child to read, one or two things will no doubt occur:

1. You will find everything is going superbly and you are more and more enthusiastic about learning more about how to teach your baby, or—
2. You may have questions or problems.

Trouble Shooting

If you have a question or have run into a problem you cannot solve, do the following:

1. Reread Chapter 7 and 8 carefully. The vast majority of all technical questions about reading are actually covered in these two chapters. You will spot what you missed the first time and be able to correct it easily. If not, go on to step 2.

2. Reread this book carefully. The vast majority of all philosophical questions about reading are covered here. Each time you

read the book you will understand it at a higher level since your experience in teaching your child will grow. You will find the answer you need; if not, go on to step 3.

3. Good teachers need a good amount of sleep. Get more sleep. Mothers, especially mothers of very young children, almost never have an adequate amount of sleep. Evaluate honestly how much sleep you get regularly. Add at least an extra hour. If this does not solve the problem, go on to step 4.

4. Get the *Glenn Doman How To Teach Your Baby To Read* Video. Information about purchasing the video can be found at the back of this book. The video will enable you to see actual demonstrations of mothers teaching their young children to read. Many mothers find this helpful. This will give you the confidence you need. If not, go on to step 5.

5. Write to us and tell us what you are doing and what your question is. We personally answer every letter and have done so since the book was first published. It may take us time to get back to you because mothers write to us from all over the world. Be certain you have *really* explored steps one through four first, but if all else fails, please write to us at The Institutes (address below).

More Information

If you want to learn more about how to teach your baby, do the following:

1. Attend the *How To Multiply Your Baby's Intelligence* Course. This is a seven-day course for mothers and fathers. Reading is only one of the many subjects that are covered. This is a wonderful course that every mother or father should attend while their children are still young or when parents are expecting a new baby. For more information, call or write to:

Course Registrar
The Institutes for the Achievement
of Human Potential
8801 Stenton Avenue
Wyndmoor, PA 19038 USA
<u>www.iahp.org</u>
Tel: (215) 233-2050

2. Read the other books in the *Gentle Revolution Series* listed in the back of this book.

3. Get the materials available in the *Gentle Revolution Series* listed in the back of this book.

4. Write to us at The Institutes and tell us what you are doing and how your child is progressing. Your information is precious to us and invaluable to future generations of mothers.

9
what mothers
say

Oh! What a power is motherhood!

—EURIPIDES

How To Teach Your Baby To Read was written in 1963 and was first published in 1964.

Forty years have passed since this book first saw the light of day. It began as a set of instructions for mothers which my wife, Katie, had agreed to actually teach the mothers providing that I wrote a precise list of instructions for her to use as a guide.

The night I began to write is permanently fixed in my memory's eye. The original intention was four or five pages of organized notes. In a very short time it was ten pages and an idea began to form. Why not actually mimeograph the notes and give each mother a copy of the notes after Katie had taught each of them? Splendid idea.

Minutes became hours and the instructions got to be twenty-five pages long. Moreover they seemed reasonably clear and reasonably readable. In fact it seemed good enough that it might be worth putting in permanent form. Perhaps it should be printed rather than mimeographed and printed as a proper lecture.

While excitement was mounting as the sentences and paragraphs fell into place and the number of pages increased, a very real worry began to intrude. A properly printed paper of this size would be expensive. It could conceivably cost hundreds of dollars. Where would we get the money? The Institutes were, and are, a nonprofit, federally tax-exempt organization. The superb professional staff existed on salaries that were so small as to be embarrassing. Would the board of directors approve such an expenditure even if we could find the money?

Excitement at what was happening conquered concern (the hope that springs eternal in the human breast) about funds and the paper was writing itself at a rapid rate.

It was long past midnight when it became clear that it was far too long to be a paper or even an article and much remained to be said. Obviously it was going to be a booklet and a rather thick one at that. Good Lord, it might cost a thousand dollars to print such a booklet. No chance the board of directors would authorize that. Even I would have had to vote against publishing such a booklet.

Hey! A booklet. Did we know somebody at a baby food company or a baby supply company that might sponsor such a booklet? Might actually pay for the whole business? What a great idea.

The possibility that we might find funds to support the booklet added to the constantly rising excitement of the writing itself, and how it would simplify the job of mothers teaching their babies to read was stimulating enough to last into the wee small hours of the morning. As the hours passed and the pages continued to grow, reality began to conquer joy. It was already too long to be a booklet. It was going to be at least fifty pages long, maybe a hundred—maybe longer. Hopes of finding the funds to print it disappeared. It was a great shame because it was both worth reading and important.

The trouble was it had actually turned out to

be, not a set of instructions or a paper or an article or a booklet as I had planned, trouble was it had actually turned into a book.

A book. A book? Holy mackerel, it was going to be a book, a book, a book! You didn't pay to have books printed—a publisher paid you.

It was early in the morning but Katie was waiting up.

"KATIE, WAIT TILL YOU HEAR. I'M WRITING A BOOK, A BOOK MIND YOU! NOT ANOTHER ARTICLE FOR PROFESSIONALS BUT A **REAL** BOOK FOR REAL PEOPLE, FOR MOTHERS AND FATHERS. WHAT DO YOU THINK OF THAT? I'LL BET THEY'LL SELL FIVE THOUSAND OF THEM!"

"Is it going to be a book to teach mothers how to teach their babies to read?" asked Katie.

It was.

Since that early morning in 1963, *How To Teach Your Baby To Read* has been published in more than twenty languages and continues to be translated into new languages.

Since that time there have been dozens of printings and reprintings.

Since that time five million parents have bought *How To Teach Your Baby To Read.*

When the original book was published there were a few hundred parents who had taught their tiny children, most of whom were brain-injured, to read. Today there are hundreds of thousands of well children as well as many thousands of brain-injured or formerly brain-injured children who can read.

How do we know that?

My most precious material possession in the world is a collection of thousands of letters from mothers (and fathers) who have written to tell us how much they have enjoyed teaching their babies to read; how much their babies have enjoyed learning to read; asking how to get additional books and materials to teach babies; asking questions about babies and to tell me what happened to their babies when they get to school and what happened to them when they grow up.

These letters constitute the greatest body of evidence in existence to prove that tiny children want to read, can learn to read, are learning to read, and should learn to read.

These letters which continue to flow in daily are so sane, so endearing, so charming, and so persuasive that they have become precious to me.

When once in a while, man's inhumanity to man seems to reach a new peak of insanity and I find myself wondering if *we* are going to survive *ourselves,* I go into my office, lock the door, and take out my letters from mothers and read them. In a very short time I am smiling, my hopes for mankind and tomorrow become a certainty, and once again it's a great day in the morning.

It seemed to me that the mothers (and fathers) reading this book might enjoy a tiny sampling of what happened to other mothers (and fathers) who had read the book earlier.

These quotes are random in the sense that each of them represents hundreds of other letters astonishingly like the one quoted.

These quotes are taken from thousands of letters. They are not selected as the most literate or the least literate, the most charming or the least charming, the most enthusiastic or the least enthusiastic, the most scientific or the least scientific, the most persuasive or the least persuasive, the most moving or the least moving. They obviously represent parents who are essentially middle-class people intellectually, educationally, and economically. They represent middle America, from blue-collar workers at one end of the middle class to professional people such as lawyers, engineers, physicians, educators, and scientists at the other.

What *all* of them have in common is that they love their children deeply and have given their children the highest priority in their lives.

These children are truly *gifted*. They are *gifted*

with parents who have both their heads and their hearts in the right place. It is perhaps the only true giftedness.

They give me the greatest hope of all.

Here, then, is a tiny sampling from the thousands of letters:

EXCERPTS OF LETTERS FROM PARENTS

Thank you very much for your book *How To Teach Your Baby To Read.* My twenty-five-month-old daughter is happily and hungrily learning to read...

Also, I don't want to stop with reading since I now realize what a marvelous little human being is in my care...

May God bless folks like you who help folks like me be a better mother, teacher, companion, and friend to my little one...

P.S. I knew I was doing the word game correctly when my husband came out of another part of our apartment to investigate all the cheering and clapping, and when my little one cried, "More words!" when we put the word game up. Here's to learning with true joy and happiness!

—Abilene, Texas

My little girl (age two and a half) is learning to read (delightedly, I might add) by the method you outline in your book. Needless to say, my husband and I are excited and happy about your work. I believe that it is the most important current development in childhood "education" that I am aware of, and as a parent I respect you highly for it. I could go on and on, but I'm sure you've heard it all before...

—Mesa, Arizona

We are parents of two children ages six years and nineteen months. My youngest child is being taught by your system. It works (and works well) and may God bless you for it...

I suppose you have been told this often enough but everyone who tries out your system cannot praise you enough. You are a much-loved man in my friends' circle...

—Maharashtra, India

I have a four-year-old boy who was so hungry for this he learned ten words on the first day and didn't want to quit to sleep—was up again at 6:00 a.m. ready to continue the next morning...

This is the happiest discovery in my career as

a mother! I only wish I had had this with my three older children (fourth, third, and first grade).

—St. Johns, Arizona

I have just finished your book, *How To Teach Your Baby To Read,* and begun teaching my seventeen-month-old daughter to read. I am so excited and enthusiastic about this project. I look at this as the greatest birthday present I could ever give her…

—Lowell, Massachusetts

You have done the "impossible." Six months ago, if someone had said that my two-year-old son could be reading by three, I would have said, "Impossible."

—New Orleans, Louisiana

Thank you so much for your innovative book, *How To Teach Your Baby To Read*—it inspired us to try it on my nephew. He is two years, three months old and he can now read more than fifty English words, some even rather difficult ones. This, only a few months after his parents tried the method with him.

This is of great significance, we believe, considering that this little boy was born, and lives, in the Philippines, where English is not the mother tongue...

—West Covina, California

I wrote you about a year ago to let you know my daughter, then two, could read about sixty words. A year has passed, and I am pleased to tell you that she is now reading books like a pro. She can read just about any book now, and she understands what she reads! I thank you for your book, *How To Teach Your Baby To Read.* I wish more mothers realized what an enjoyable experience it is for small children to learn. My daughter, Josie, I believe, reads much better than kids four years older (or even older!)

...I am very grateful to be able to help my daughter learn. She enjoys it thoroughly, and she asks me to please "play school" with her. Indeed, kids love to learn.

—Covington, Louisiana

I first read *How To Teach Your Baby To Read* when our son was fourteen months old. We got a slow start into it, getting all the materials together, etc. But, at eighteen months, my son started to speak clearly and I finally began to realize that he was retaining it all! Terrific! We are real excited about it all! Thank you for opening our minds.

—Falls Church, Virginia

I employed your method on my granddaughter at age two and she could read the *Reader's Digest* at age three. Currently she is an "A" student in Los Angeles schools at age sixteen. I recommend your book to all young mothers. Thanks...

—Escondido, California

I have read your book entitled *How To Teach Your Baby To Read* and am thoroughly delighted with the results I've had with my thirty-five-month-old daughter. I began teaching her only four days ago and she is grasping the words at a phenomenal rate! Of course I may be prejudiced since she is my daughter, but this program is really exciting!

—Orem, Utah

...I started this program with my twin boys when they were two years old. They are now thirteen years and always at the head of their class. In fact, they have been placed by the schools in a class for "gifted" children. They were reading fluently and with understanding by three years, and were writing by four. This experience was one of the most rewarding ones I have had in raising our sons.

—Maple Ridge, British Columbia

When my daughter was about one year old, I saw a program from The Institutes which showed brain "deficient" children who could read and babies who could recognize specific numbers of dots. I attempted to use the techniques shown with my baby. She learned to read words at age two, read sentences by three, and whole books by four.

—East Stroudsburg, Pennsylvania

I wanted to thank you so much for opening an exciting world to my children.

When my son, Aaron, was three years old, I read your book *How To Teach Your Baby To Read*. Very suspiciously I began the program you outlined. Six months later, Aaron was reading a vast amount of vocabulary words. But much more to my surprise, his sister (one and a half) had learned right along with him. She picked up the words one day and one by one read through all of them. Today (five years later) my children are doing great! They love school, they love to learn. Trisha (almost seven) has written two of her own books as well as many single stories. Thank you so much for your research and your book.

—Newberg, Oregon

I'm writing to tell you that my personal experience has been marvelous. I started the program with my then twenty-six-month-old daughter in February. By the end of March, she was reading [the book] "Good-Bye Mommy." Now, at thirty-four and a half months she reads everything and anything in sight. She can sound out words as well as almost any of the fifth-graders I had during ten years of teaching.

—Omaha, Nebraska

We successfully taught our first son to read at an early age, using your book, *How To Teach Your Baby To Read.* Last May, in first grade, he tested first in his class, with a fourth-grade reading and comprehension level.

I must tell you that I received a copy of your

book as a joke, since I read quite a bit.

My family really laughed when I used the methods on my nineteen-month-old son. But the laughing stopped when he read books at two and a half.

Our only problem came up when we were traveling and our son could read the fast food billboards and wanted to stop at every one!

—Piketon, Ontario

Eight years ago, I happened upon your book *How To Teach Your Baby To Read* and decided to try your methods on my then three-year-old daughter. It was a total success in spite of my hit-or-miss approach, and she's been reading up a storm ever since.

When my second daughter was born, I was determined to do it right from start to finish but while my intentions were good, time was short, and she got an even briefer version than number one. Once again it took, and she, like her sister, was reading earlier and more competently than anyone else around.

By the time my son came along I was totally convinced, and he is now four and amazes everyone with his skill. It has been an extremely satisfying experience for me each time and I would not have missed the moment when it all came together for each of my children, for all the money in the world. Thank you.

—Petaluma, California

My father, three years ago, bought me Glenn Doman's *How To Teach Your Baby To Read* and life hasn't been the same since. He (my son) loves reading—our Friday shopping expedition takes us to the library where he spends ages reading away to himself, while I wander around supermarkets feeling sorry for mothers dragging reluctant youngsters round with them.

This week's books included words like "infuriating," "irreplaceable," and "paraphernalia," all of which gave him very little bother...

—Benfleet, Essex, England

My son, Jason, was born in 1976 and being a single parent I lived with a group of nuns who helped me raise my son for the first couple years. The nuns had six to eight babies to look after during the day. They also had your book *How To Teach Your Baby To Read* and the flip cards that went with the book. They'd line up all the babies in their chairs and show the flip cards as well as a pile of flip cards the nuns had made themselves in short intervals, four to five times a day. The babies loved it and they all learned how to read, including my baby, Jason.

He's twenty-five years old now and a proud father of a baby boy. Jason wants me to find a package of flip cards like the nuns used.* Do you still sell them? I also wanted to take this opportunity to thank you for being so intelligent and recognizing years ago that it's best to teach babies how to read. Thank you.

—British Columbia, Canada

I took your courses* in 1982 and in 1986. I loved every moment. What I received from you people was worth millions...

I always said (since the time they were born) that I wanted my children to grow up to be decent people, who knew how to deal with their fellow man *and* contribute something. My sons chose not to complete college. They were both A+ students, but they did not want to further their education. However, they are very decent people.

My one son is absolutely a social genius! He can talk to anyone about anything. He always makes everyone feel comfortable and welcome. I have never seen anyone like him. *Everyone* I meet that knows him tells me what a very special young man (now twenty-one) he is. He works in a bank, investments. I could tell you about his achievements in his job, but it's not important.

My older son has just made me a grand-mother. Now the Bits* and other materials come out of storage for my precious grand-daughter... [His wife] told me that she thanks God every day that I raised him the way that I did because he is a beautiful person. She never knew anyone like him. His mother-in-law spoke to me from 3,000 miles away and said she had to meet the person who raised such a beauti-ful person.

All of you helped me reach my goals. I can-not tell you that they are Nobel Prize winners, rocket scientists, or even "successful financially" in the eyes of the world. But they are decent, responsible, loving, caring, giving people who contribute to those whose lives they touch.

I often think of you, with such tender feel-ings and such tender tears. What I learned from The Institutes did truly change my life, and I thank you forever.

—Desert Hot Springs, California

I have just finished reading your new book *How To Multiply Your Baby's Intelligence.** I can-not tell you how glad I am that you have written this book. You clearly deserve a Nobel Prize.

It was over twenty years ago that I bought a copy of *How To Teach Your Baby To Read* and promptly taught my three children to read long before school. The results were (and are) very impressive. I advocated the concept (and still do) to friends who have small children. I put on demos with my kids and even gave away a few copies of your book. Yet, as far as I know, no one else taught his baby to read. I suppose I know some of the frustration that you feel. As Winston Churchill once said, "Men occasionally stumble on the truth, but most of them pick themselves up and hurry off as if nothing happened."

My daughter Katherine…is now a student at Bryn Mawr. She was a National Merit Scholarship Finalist and she won a national poetry contest at the age of twelve.

I am now teaching my youngest daughter, Bethany, age one. No doubt a better job will be done due to your new book.

—Fort Washington, Maryland

Our association with you and the Evan Thomas Institute has provided my wife and me with many opportunities to work with our son [two years and ten months old] and our new daughter, Alexis [four months], at a most precious time in their life…

Alexandre is being considered by Columbia University for enrollment in their gifted children's program. Since only fourteen children are admitted to the program out of thousands of applicants, he was required to take the Stanford-Binet I.Q. test, which was administered by the testing center of Columbia's choice.

The psychologist commented that his I.Q. is well above 160 but the test could not measure beyond 160. He also commented that Alexandre was beyond a doubt the brightest child he had personally ever tested (the psychologist has been testing children for many years). It goes without saying that he will continue with the Evan Thomas Institute Off-Campus Program in any event and we consider this the far more important program. We are convinced that the I.Q. is a direct result of your techniques and programs.

Please accept my thanks and best wishes for your continued good health and search for the understanding and development of children.

—New York, New York

COMPLETE LETTERS
FROM PARENTS

Please forgive me if somehow I feel I know you personally. Please allow me now to say "Hello" after many years of thinking about you and your work at The Institutes for the Achievement of Human Potential. The fact is I feel that whatever words I might write would be inadequate to express the gratitude and thanks I owe for the words in that book *(How To Teach Your Baby To Read)* and the discoveries you and your team have made and described so well.

I first came across your book in 1972, shortly after my son was born. It was in W. H. Smith's bookshop in Southampton on the south coast of England. In 1973 we moved to the island of Mauritius in the Indian Ocean. There, on the clear sandy beaches and in the shade of the bouganvillea, we taught him to read following your methods. At three years old he could quite happily read P.D. Eastman's "Going to the Moon." My parents-in-law complained bitterly when we returned to England that year that too much time was being spent reading before bedtime and that he was too young. At seven he had a reading age of eleven, and at thirteen he won a full-fees scholarship to Harrow, to the great surprise and pleasure of many members of a large extended family. His seventeenth birthday is in July.

We also used your methods with my two daughters, whose pleasure in reading and love of books is a joy to behold.

May I also say that February of this year my wife, Jennifer, took up teaching the possibly brain-injured child of a friend using your methods after the school inspector said the child should spend the next six months "learning" the letter **C**. Anyone can see the intelligence shining in the young Anna Ross's blue eyes. She's five years old.

The secretary in the office where I work has a son aged fifteen months and she is now having a marvelous time teaching him to read.

Jennifer and I believe your methods could help Anna Ross improve enormously in neurological organization and enable the young child to keep up with her elder brother and younger sister, or maybe, one dares hope, surpass them.

Thank you, sir, enormously, for the great work and power of your discoveries and the benefits they have bestowed upon my family.

—Taunton, England

My first contact with your materials was in 1963 when my younger brother was born. My mother read your book (hot off the press) and made a bet with my dad that she could teach her baby to read. Ken was reading many words from seeing them on the television very early. We (three sisters) all helped play the word games. Mom wrote words on the blackboard in our kitchen, and she cut up the cardboards that came in my dad's shirts from the cleaners and wrote words on them. His baby book records that he could read fifty-five words by his second birthday, and he could read almost anything by his third. He enjoyed writing as a young child and penned many little books, complete with illustrations.

When Ken was in elementary school I was in high school, and I began teaching him some elements of algebra and geometry. He competed on math teams in high school and excels in math to this day. It would fill a book if I reiterated all my brother's pursuits and accomplishments as a child. I am convinced that it was the result of early education. Ken has won a number of honors and awards, was second in his class in high school, and is presently on an academic scholarship in university where he is an engineering student. He was (and is) very well adjusted socially also.

Now I have a little girl of my own. Madeline is two, and I am using both your reading and math materials* with her. I also read *Kindergar-*

ten is Too Late and was inspired to expose Madeline to all sorts of things: classical music, drawing and painting, gymnastics, geography, films, the Bible, swimming, and numerous other learning experiences.

She has a large collection of puzzles and loves to sit for long periods of time working on them. She's learning the states through her U.S. map puzzles, countries of the world on flash cards, U.S. Presidents on flash cards, etc. She is a delightful child with excellent verbal ability, a quick mind, and quite a sense of humor! I will admit to you privately that I have observed that she is far more advanced than other children her age, and people comment on that all the time.

—Dallas, Texas

I have read with considerable interest your letter on the subject of teaching one's baby to read. This brought many pleasant memories back to both my husband and myself, and I brought out your book, *How To Teach Your Baby To Read*, and noted the date was October 26, 1964. At that time our son, Keith, was sixteen months old. Just prior to obtaining your book we had read an article covering your work at The Institutes for the Achievement of Human

Potential on this same subject. With great enthusiasm, my husband and I set out to teach Keith to read. We printed our cards initially—quite a few of them—and launched the program when Keith was seventeen months old. The results were absolutely "mind boggling."

Today Keith is nineteen years old, having graduated from St. Francis College as Valedictorian of his class in Chemistry and Biology at age fifteen years. He has been attending Indiana University as a double medical major and science student (combined M.D./Ph.D.) and will receive his Ph.D. degree a year from now (age twenty); two years later he will receive his M.D. and then will continue to specialize in whatever medical field he chooses.

To say we have enjoyed Keith's accomplishments immensely would be a gross understatement. There is no doubt that his ability to read early has done much to enhance his progress throughout the years; and incidentally, socially he is a well-adjusted person—has never had any serious problem in dealing with his peers, who have always been five to seven years older than Keith. He has always been accepted well by his classmates, teachers, and professional associates.

He is an accomplished organist—having built a full-size theatre organ at age nine—and also an accomplished guitarist and singer with his own folk group at St. Paul's Catholic Church in Bloomington (Indiana University Campus), Indiana.

In view of your obvious delight in success stories that help take your depression away, perhaps this one might add a little light to your soul as well.

We would be delighted to hear from you and, in a sense, you might consider Keith as one of your products. I am sure you would find it a joy to meet him some day.

P.S. Keith is at the top of his entering medical class for the fourth year with all "A's".

—Ft. Wayne, Indiana

In 1964 my father imported what was probably one of the few copies of *How To Teach Your Baby To Read* into Ireland in order to begin my education. I was six months old at the time and went through the entire reading program and one of generally accelerated learning organized by my parents.

Thirty-five years later I find myself beginning my own child's education program and have gravitated to your publications as the basis for a learning program for Mia, our little girl.

I thought I would write to you since my selection was not done on the basis of any conscious awareness of your books. (My parents never told me what materials and references they used to educate me and my brothers.)

My choice of your program was on the basis of a subconscious comfort with the picture on the front of the *How To Teach Your Baby To Read* book. I reacted warmly to the flash card image depicted on it. When I told my parents of my choice of your book they then told me of how they had chosen the same materials.

I just thought you would be interested to hear of the deep and positive memories which your teaching method had generated.

I would also be interested to hear of any direction you could provide for source material for the Encyclopedic Knowledge* program, which I would like to develop for Mia over the next year.

—North Sydney, Australia

I was one of the early "Doman" mothers. In 1965 I was an unenthusiastic expectant mother until March and April of that year, when I read an article in *Ladies' Home Journal* entitled "How to Teach Your Baby to be a Genius." The moment I read the article it was like the Green Flash of Revelation! It opened up a brilliant and vast horizon, and I could hardly wait for the day I could begin to lead my child down this wondrous path. I enjoyed the process of making the reading cards, finding it relaxing and serene. During Heather's first four years of life we moved from the U.S. to Chile, Peru, and Brazil, and wherever we went a supply of white poster board and red felt pens went along. When delays in shipping held things up, words were written on steamed-up windows or in the sand on the beach, and Heather was bilingual in English and Spanish, later adding French beginning in Grade One in Canada. How I wish we had also had the math program* at the time!

I went to school in England almost sixty years ago and my husband attended school in Canada, and neither of us can remember any child being unable to read no matter what their economic background might be. Even in the poorest (financially) homes there was an old maiden aunt or grannie who took pride in teaching the children their "letters," as they would say. Recently, my husband had his first experience of a young man in his mid-twenties, a high school graduate who could not read or write. Truly, when the day comes and I stand before my "Maker" and am called to account I shall be able to say that my greatest contribution was teaching my child to read.

Sincere good wishes for the continued work of The Institutes, and my heartfelt thanks for opening up the wonderful world of childhood.

—Honolulu, Hawaii

We bought your book *How To Teach Your Baby To Read* in 1964, when our firstborn was two years old. It worked like a charm. He was reading at the fifth-grade level in the first grade, excelled in every subject in every grade, found music lessons easy, won every math contest entered, and received 1400-plus on his SAT exam.

At seventeen he went to UC Berkeley and graduated Phi Beta Kappa in physics. Later he earned an M.S. from UCLA, where he was awarded a fellowship. He is now teaching college and is a resource person on English usage for the curriculum committee. My wife and I are not particularly smart, and I've always thought that early reading skills were what made all the difference. I have just bought all your reading and math books* for my new granddaughter. Thanks for such a fine thing.

P.S. My son represented California in the National Spelling Bee in 1973 and 1974.

—Gig Harbor, Washington

Twenty-six years ago, I bought your book *How To Teach Your Baby To Read.* My husband and I began an exciting adventure with our son, John, and six years later continued with our daughter, Christa.

John's birth history was not the best. I developed toxemia, was put on bed rest, and after thirty-three hours of labor John was born. The umbilical cord was wrapped around his neck, his right lung did not inflate, and he immediately developed pneumonia. The ob-gyn doctor told me several times that John came "this close" to being mentally retarded.

John walked early, at nine months, but talked late, after he was two years old. John was probably fifteen months old when we began your program. He never resisted, in fact, he frequently would get the cards and bring them to me. By John's third birthday he could read everything. When tested in the public school system before entering kindergarten, John was reading on the third-grade level. Also at that time, he was diagnosed as having minimal brain dysfunction. Due to his advanced skills and outstanding test scores, we were advised to move and put John in a private school where he could get the attention he so deserved. We did.

John graduated from high school and went on to Stanford University, where he graduated with honors and distinction with a major in political science, completing all necessary requirements in three years. He then went to the University of Michigan Law School, made Law Review, and was courted by the finest law firms in the United States. He now practices corporate law in San Francisco. He has been a lifelong reader. It is indeed one of his favorite pastimes.

Our next child was adopted at the age of four months from Korea. We know almost nothing about her birth history. Again the cards came out, and at the age of three Christa read anything and everything.

Her second-grade class made a contract to read thirty books by the end of the year. Christa met her quota by October and read 360 books that year. She sailed through lower, middle, and high school and was accepted at the College of William and Mary, where again she excels and will graduate this May with a major in finance. Both children's lives were influenced greatly by your work and we are forever in your debt. My husband and I offer you our most sincere thanks. Please contact me at any time for additional information.

—Phoenix, Maryland

---

*Information about courses, books, kits, and teaching materials can be found in the back of this book.

10
on joyousness

*I don't think we really got to know
each other until we played the
learning-to-read game together.*

—MANY, MANY MOTHERS

For many generations grandparents have been advising their sons and daughters to enjoy their children because, they have warned, all too soon the children will be grown up and gone. Like much good advice that has been passed on from one generation to another, it is rarely heeded until it has happened. When it has happened it is, of course, too late to do anything about it.

If it is true that the parents of brain-injured

children have monumental problems (and they certainly do), it is equally true that they have certain advantages that the parents of well children rarely have. Not the least of these advantages is the fact that they have a very intimate relationship with their children. By the nature of the illness it is sometimes an agonizing one, but it is also a precious one.

Recently, during a course we were presenting to the parents of well children on the subject of how to teach your baby to read, we said in passing, "And another excellent reason for teaching your baby to read is the fact that in the close relationship required you will experience a great deal of the joy that the parents of brain-injured children know in dealing with their children."

It was not until several sentences further along that we became aware of the puzzled looks that our comments had produced.

It is not surprising that parents of well children are not aware of the fact that the parents of brain-injured children have some advantages and not only problems. It is surprising, however, that the vast majority of us have lost the constant and intimate relationship with our children that is so important to the child's entire future and which can be so splendidly pleasurable to us.

The pressures of our society and of our culture have robbed us of this so quietly that we have been unaware of the fact that it is gone, or perhaps we have been unaware that it ever existed.

It did exist, and it is worth recapturing. One of the most rewarding ways to recapture this joyous association is by teaching your baby to read.

Now that you know how to do it, let's finish off with some final reminders—some dos and some don'ts.

Let's begin with the don'ts.

Don't bore your child.

It is the cardinal sin. Remember that the two-year-old could be learning Portuguese and French along with the English he is learning so well. So don't bore him with trivia and drivel. There are two easy ways to bore him. Avoid them like the plague.

1. *Going too slow.* This will bore him, because he will learn at a surprising rate. Many people commit this sin in their desire to be quite positive he knows the material.

2. *Testing*. This is the most likely sin and this will surely bore him. Children love to learn but they do not love to be tested. This is the primary reason why all the commotion is called for after he has tested successfully.

Two factors precipitate toward too much testing. The first of these is the naturally proud parent showing off the child's abilities to neighbors, cousins, grandparents, and so on. The second factor is the parent's keen desire to be sure he reads each word perfectly before moving on to the next step. Remember that you are not giving your child college board examinations, you're simply giving him an opportunity to learn to read. It is not necessary to prove to the world that he can read. (He'll prove it all by himself later on.) Only *you* need be sure, and parents have special, built-in equipment for knowing what their children know and what they don't. Trust that equipment and the judgment it hands down. That special equipment is made up of equal portions of head and heart, and when both of these things are in total accord you get a good verdict almost invariably.

We shall not soon forget a conversation with an outstanding pediatric neurosurgeon who was discussing a severely brain-injured child. The brain surgeon was a man whose every instinct was based on deliberate, almost cold-blooded scientific evidence.

He was talking about a fifteen-year-old severely brain-injured child, paralyzed and speechless, who had been diagnosed as an idiot. The doctor was furious. "Look at this child," he insisted. "He has been diagnosed as an idiot simply because he looks like an idiot, acts like an idiot, and the laboratory tests indicate that he is an idiot. Anyone should be able to see that he is not an idiot."

There was a long, embarrassed, somewhat frightened silence among the residents, interns, nurses, and therapists who composed the brain surgeon's retinue. Finally a resident, bolder than the rest, said, "But, Doctor, if everything indicates that this child is an idiot, how do you know that he isn't?"

"Good God," roared the scientist-surgeon, "look at his eyes, man. You don't need any special training to see the intelligence shining in them!"

A year later we were privileged to watch that child walk, talk, and read for the same group of people.

There are accurate ways for parents to know what a child knows outside of the realm of the ordinary tests.

If you repeat too often a test which a child has already passed, he will become bored and will reply by telling you he doesn't know or by giving you an absurd answer. If you show a child the word "hair" and ask him too often what it is, he may tell you that it is "elephant." When he replies in this way your child is straightening you out by reproof. Pay attention to him.

Don't pressure your child.

Don't cram reading down his throat. Don't be *determined* to teach him to read. Don't be afraid of failure. (How can you fail? If he only learns three words he will be better off than if he knows none at all.) You must *not* give him the opportunity to learn to read if either one of you doesn't feel like doing it. Teaching a child to read is a very positive thing and you must never make it negative. If the child doesn't want to play at any time during the learning process, put the whole thing away for a week or so. Remember you have absolutely nothing to lose and everything to gain.

Don't be tense.

If you are not relaxed, don't play the game by attempting to cover up your tension. A child is the most sensitive instrument imaginable. He will know that you are tense and that will subtly convey unpleasantness to him. It is much better to waste a day or a week. Never try to fool the child. You won't succeed.

Be joyous.

We have said earlier in this book that thousands of parents and scientists have taught children to read and that the results have been splendid.

We have read about these people, we have corresponded with many of these people, and we have talked to many of them. We have found that the methods they employ have varied widely. They have used materials ranging from pencil and paper to complex scientific machines that are very expensive. However, and most significantly, each of the methods about which we have learned had three things in common, and they are of the utmost importance.

1. Each method used in teaching tiny children to read was successful.
2. Each of them used large print.
3. Each of them stressed the absolute necessity for feeling and expressing joyousness in the process.

The first two points surprised us not at all, but the third point astonished us.

It must be remembered that the many people teaching children to read were unaware of one another, and that they were often generations apart.

It is not just a coincidence that all of them came to the conclusion that a child should be rewarded for his success by lavish praise. They would have had to come to that conclusion sooner or later.

What is truly astonishing is that people working in 1914, 1918, 1962, and 1963, and in other times and far-flung places, should all have come to the conclusion that this attitude should be summed up in a single, identical word—*joyous.*

To almost the precise degree that a parent's attitude is joyous will he succeed in teaching his child to read. There was a strong temptation to title this final chapter of the book "The Dizzy Blondes," and thereby hangs a brief but important tale.

Through the years, we at The Institutes have gained a vast respect for mothers. Like most people we have erred by making easy generalizations and have therefore, at least for convenience, divided into two categories the thousands of mothers with whom we have had the privilege of dealing. The first category is a relatively small group of highly intellectual, highly educated, very calm, very quiet, and generally, but not invariably, intelligent mothers. This group we have termed "the intellectuals."

The second group is by far the largest and includes almost everybody else. While these women are often intelligent, they are inclined to be less intellectual and a good deal more enthusiastic than the first. This group of mothers we have called "the dizzy blondes," which reflects their enthusiasm rather than the color of their hair or their intelligence.

Like all generalizations the above doesn't hold up, but it does make for rapid grouping.

When we first became aware that mothers could teach their tiny children to read and that this was a fine thing to do we said to each other, "Wait till our mothers hear about this." We anticipated correctly that all of our mothers would be delighted and that they would tackle this process with enthusiasm.

We came to the conclusion that the vast majority of mothers would be successful in teaching their children to read, but we predicted that the small group of intellectuals would enjoy even more success than "the dizzy blondes."

When the first results began to come in, almost exactly the opposite of what we had anticipated proved to be the case. All later results confirmed and reconfirmed our initial findings.

All of the mothers had succeeded beyond our initial expectations but "the dizzy blondes" were well ahead of the intellectuals, and the dizzier the mother the more she accomplished.

When we examined the results, watched the process, listened to the mother, and thought about it all for a while, the reasons for the whole thing became obvious.

When the quiet, serious mother taught her child she was inclined to do so in a quiet, serious way.

On the other hand, the more relaxed mothers were a great deal more inclined to shout "Wow, That's great!" These were the mothers who showed by voice, motion, and commotion their elation and joy in teaching their child.

Again the answer was simple. Tiny children understand, appreciate, and go for "Wow!" Children love celebrations—so give them what they want. They deserve it and so do you.

There are so many things we parents *must* do for our children. We must take care of all of their problems, the occasional large serious ones and the innumerable smaller ones. Both the kids and we are entitled to our joy, and that's just what teaching them to read is— a joy.

But if the idea of teaching your child to read doesn't appeal to you, don't do it. No one should teach her child to read just for the sake of keeping up with the Joneses. If you feel that way, you'll be a bad teacher. If you want to do it, then do it because you want to—that's a splendid reason.

If we must deal with all the problems our children have, then we should also have the pleasures that go with this instead of turning such opportunities for happiness over to strangers. What a privilege it is to open for a child a door that has behind it all of the golden words of excitement, splendor, and wonder that are contained in the books of the English language. That's much too good to be turned over to a stranger. That joyous privilege should be reserved for Mom or Dad.

Be inventive.

Long ago we learned that if you tell mothers what the objective is in any project related to their kids, and if you then tell them in general how it should be done, you can stop worrying about it right then and there. Parents are extraordinarily inventive and as long as they know what the limits are, they will often come up with better methods than they have been told to use.

Every child shares many characteristics with all other children (and chief among them is the ability to learn to read at a very early age), but every child is also very much an individual. He is a product of his family, his life, and his home. Because they are all different, there are many small games that Mother can and will invent to make learning to read more fun for her child. Obey the rules, but go ahead and add things that you know will work particularly well for your child. Don't be afraid to tamper within the framework of rules which have been set forth here.

Answer all of the child's questions.

He will have a thousand questions. Answer them seriously and as accurately as you can. You opened a large door when you taught him to read. Don't be surprised at the vast number of things which will interest him. The most common question you will hear from now on is, "What is this word?" That's how he'll learn to read all the books from now on. Always tell him what that word is. His basic reading vocabulary will grow at a very rapid rate if you do.

Give him worthwhile material to read.

There are so many magnificent things to read that there should be very little time devoted to junk.

Perhaps the most important thing overall is that reading gives you the opportunity to spend more time in personal, close, and intriguing contact with your child. Take advantage of every opportunity to be with your child. Modern living has tended to pull mothers and children apart. Here is the perfect chance to get together. The mutual love, respect, and admiration which will grow greater through such contact is worth many, many times over the small amounts of time which you will have to spend.

It seems worthwhile to finish by speculating briefly on what all this could mean to the future.

All through history man has had two dreams. The first of these dreams, and the simpler, has been to change the world around us for the better. We have succeeded in doing this to a fantastic degree.

At the turn of the twentieth century man could travel no faster than a little over a hundred miles per hour. Today he is capable of flying through space at more than 17,000 miles per hour. We have developed miracle drugs which will double man's life span. We have learned how to project our voices and our images through space by radio, television, and the internet. Our buildings are truly miracles of height, beauty, warmth, and comfort. We have changed the world around us in the most extraordinary way.

But what of man himself? He lives longer because he has invented better medicine. He grows taller because the transportation he has invented brings him a greater variety of food, and therefore nutrition, from distant places.

But is man himself better? Are there people of greater imaginative genius than da Vinci? Are there better writers than Shakespeare? Are there people with further vision and broader knowledge than Franklin and Jefferson?

Since time immemorial there have been men who fostered the second dream. For ages some human beings have dared to ask the question, "But what of man himself?" As the world around us daily grows more breathtakingly complex, we have need for a new, better, and wiser breed of *Homo sapiens*.

People have, of necessity, grown more specialized and narrow. There is no longer time enough to know everything. Yet ways must be found to cope with the situation, to give more people the opportunity of gaining the tremendous amount of knowledge man has accumulated.

We cannot solve this problem by going to school forever. Who will run the world or be the breadwinner?

Making man live longer doesn't really help this particular problem. If even a genius like Einstein had lived five years longer, would he have contributed much more to the world's knowledge? It is unlikely. Longevity does not contribute to creativity.

The answer to this problem may already have occurred to you. Suppose more children were introduced to the great storehouse of knowledge accumulated by man four or five years earlier then they are now? Imagine the result if Einstein could have had five extra years of creative life. Imagine what might happen if children could begin to absorb the wisdom and knowledge of the world, years before they are now allowed to?

What a race and what a future might we not produce if we could stop the tragic waste of children's lives when their ability to take in language in all forms is at its peak.

Certainly it is no longer a question whether very young children can read or not, it is now only a question of what they are going to read.

The real question, we guess, now that the secret is out, is a new one. Now that the kids can read and thus increase their knowledge, perhaps beyond anybody's wildest dreams—what will they do with this old world and how tolerant will they be with us old parents, who by their standards may be nice—but perhaps not very bright?

It was said long ago, and said wisely, that the pen is mightier than the sword. We must, I think, accept the belief that knowledge leads to greater understanding and thus to greater good, while ignorance inevitably leads to evil.

Little children have begun to read and thus to increase their knowledge, and if this book leads to only one child reading sooner and better, then it will have been worth the effort. Who can say what another superior child will mean to the world? Who is to say what, in the end, will be the sum total of good for man as a result of this quiet groundswell which has already begun, this gentle revolution.

acknowledgments

Nobody ever writes a book all by himself; behind every work stretches a long line of the people who made it possible. In the immediate past these people are in sharp focus, but as the line gets farther back the image of those who contributed gets dimmer and is finally totally obscured by the fog of time itself. Others go unsung, since many who have contributed to an idea have themselves passed into total obscurity.

Surely the lineal descent of this work passes back into time dimly seen and must include those who contributed even a single sentence or idea which helped complete the puzzle. It must finally include a host of mothers who knew in their hearts and minds that their children could do more than the world believed possible.

In short, in addition to those here acknowledged individually I wish to acknowledge all those in history who have believed with a consuming passion that children were really quite superior to the image that we adults have always held.

Among these many I acknowledge:

Dr. Temple Fay, a dean of neurosurgeons, who had a monumental curiosity and a unique ability to question whether accepted "truths" were true or not, and who first set us afire.

Mary Blackburn, the eternal secretary, who lived for the Children's Clinic and who, it may be said, died for it.

Dr. Eugene Spitz, pediatric neurosurgeon, who believed that "there is no more radical an act than watching a child die, knowing he is going to die, and doing nothing about it." He did so much about it.

Dr. Robert Doman, pediatric physiatrist and Medical Director of The Institutes for the Achievement of Human Potential, who wanted us to look at every single child as unique.

Dr. Raymundo Veras, physiatrist of Brazil, who returned to teach the teachers.

Dr. Carl Delacato, Director of The Institute of Reading Disability, who kept us ever mindful of the children.

Dr. Edward B. LeWinn, Director of The Research Institute, who insisted that we look at cerebrospinal fluid for the evidence we needed.

Florence Scott, R.N., who cared so much about children and who talked to them in a unique way.

Lindley Boyer, Director of The Rehabilitation Center at Philadelphia, who never stopped pushing to get our work done.

Greta Erdtmann, executive secretary, who gave me seclusion when I needed it.

Betty Milliner, whose work was exacting.

Behind all this team there have been those who cared and supported us through the days of obscurity and quest:

Helen Clarke, Herbert Thiel, Dora Kline Valentine, Gene Brog, Lloyd Wells, Frank McCormick, Robert Magee, Hugh Clarke, Gilbert Clarke, Harry Valentine, Edward and Dorothy Cassard, General Arthur Kemp, Hannah Cooke, Frank Cliffe, Chatham Wheat, Anthony Flores, Trimble Brown, Adjutant General of Pennsylvania Thomas R. White, Jr., Edward and Pat O'Donnell, Theodore Donahue, Harold McCuen, John and Mary Begley, Claude Cheek, Martin Palmer, Signe Brunnstromm, Agnes Seymour, Betty Marsh, Dr. Walter McKinney, Judge Summerill, George Leyrer, Raymond Schwartz, Ralph Rosenberg, Charlotte Kornbluh, Alan Emlen, David Taylor, Brooke Simcox, William Reimer, Emily Abell, Doris Magee, Joseph Barnes, Norma Hoffman, Tom and Sidney Carroll, Bea Lipp, Miles and Stuart Valentine, Morton Berman, John Gurt, and a host of others.

The Medical Advisory Board who have, to a man, supported the work. The following physicians who have contributed to and wholeheartedly supported the work:

Dr. Thaine Billingsley, Dr. Charles DeLone, Dr. Paul Dunn, Dr. David Lozow, Dr. William

Ober, Dr. Robert Tentler, Dr. Myron Segal, and Dr. Richard Darnell.

My children Bruce, Janet, and Douglas, who have contributed both inspirationally and materially to this book.

Cathy Ruhling, who has lovingly typed the manuscript for every book I have ever written, including this one.

Robert Loomis, my editor at Random House, who dealt with me patiently and tactfully.

Janet Gauger, my editor for this third edition at The Gentle Revolution Press. She left no stone unturned to make sure that the book was exactly the way we wanted it to be.

Last of all I acknowledge those superb teachers, the children, who have taught me most of all, especially Tommy Lunski and Walter Rice.

about the
authors

GLENN DOMAN received his degree in physical therapy from the University of Pennsylvania in 1940. From that point on, he began pioneering the field of child brain development. In 1955, he founded The Institutes for the Achievement of Human Potential in Philadelphia.

By the early sixties, the world-renowned work of The Institutes with brain-injured children had led to vital discoveries about the growth and development of well children. The author has lived with, studied, and worked with children in more than 100 nations, ranging from the most civilized to the most primitive. The Brazilian government knighted him for his outstanding work on behalf of the children of the world.

Glenn Doman is the international best-selling author of the Gentle Revolution Series, consisting of *How To Teach Your Baby To Read, How To Teach Your Baby Math, How To Multiply Your Baby's Intelligence, How To Give Your Baby Encyclopedic Knowledge,* and *How To Teach Your Baby To Be Physically Superb.* He is also the author of *What*

To Do About Your Brain-Injured Child, a guide for parents of hurt children. Currently, he continues to devote all of his time to teaching parents of both hurt and well children.

For over forty years Glenn Doman and the child brain developmentalists of The Institutes have been demonstrating that very young children are far more capable of learning than we ever imagined. He has taken this remarkable work—work that explores why children from birth to age six learn better and faster than older children do—and given it practical application. As the founder of The Institutes for the Achievement of Human Potential, he has created a comprehensive early development program that any parent can follow at home.

When Glenn Doman decided to update the books of the Gentle Revolution Series, it was only natural that his daughter help him to edit and organize the additional information gained since some of the books were first written.

JANET DOMAN is the director of The Institutes for the Achievement of Human Potential and Glenn's daughter.

After completing studies in zoology at the University of Hull in England and physical anthropology at the University of Pennsylvania, she devoted herself to teaching early reading programs to parents at The Institutes.

She spent almost two years at the Early Development Association in Japan, where she created programs for mothers. From there she returned to Philadelphia to direct the Evan Thomas Institute, a unique school for mothers and babies. The Early Development Program led to the creation of the International School for children who graduated from the Early Development Program.

Janet spends most of her day nose-to-nose with "the best parents in the world," helping them to discover the vast potential of their babies and their own potential as teachers.

In addition, she has helped her father update his historic books.

index

appendix

COURSES
offered at The Institutes for the Achievement of Human Potential

**HOW TO MULTIPLY YOUR BABY'S INTELLIGENCE®
COURSE**

**WHAT TO DO ABOUT YOUR BRAIN-INJURED CHILD™
COURSE**

---

*For information regarding these courses,
please contact:*

**The Institutes for the Achievement
of Human Potential
8801 Stenton Avenue
Wyndmoor, PA 19038 USA**

www.iahp.org

**PHONE: 215-233-2050
FAX: 215-233-3940
Toll-Free: 800-344-6684
E-Mail: institutes@iahp.org**

RELATED BOOKS, VIDEOS & KITS
IN THE GENTLE REVOLUTION SERIES

HOW TO TEACH YOUR BABY TO READ
Glenn Doman and Janet Doman

How To Teach Your Baby To Read provides your child with the enjoyment of reading. It shows you just how easy and pleasurable it is to teach a young child to read. It explains how to begin and expand the reading program, how to make and organize your materials, and how to more fully develop your child's potential.

Also available: **How To Teach Your Baby To Read**™ **Video**
How To Teach Your Baby To Read™ **Kits**
How To Teach Your Baby To Read™
    Audio Lectures

HOW TO TEACH YOUR BABY MATH
Glenn Doman and Janet Doman

How To Teach Your Baby Math instructs you in successfully developing your child's ability to think and reason. It shows you just how easy and pleasurable it is to teach a young child math. It explains how to begin and expand the math program, how to make and organize your materials, and how to more fully develop your child's potential.

Also available: **How To Teach Your Baby Math**™ **Video**
How To Teach Your Baby Math™ **Kits**
How To Teach Your Baby Math™
    Audio Lectures

HOW TO GIVE YOUR BABY ENCYCLOPEDIC KNOWLEDGE
Glenn Doman, Janet Doman, and Susan Aisen

How To Give Your Baby Encyclopedic Knowledge provides a program of visually stimulating information designed to help your child take advantage of his or her natural potential to learn anything. It shows you just how easy and pleasurable it is to teach a young child about the arts, science, and nature. Your child will recognize the insects in the garden, know the countries of the world, discover the beauty of a painting by van Gogh, and more. It explains how to begin and expand your program, how to make and organize your materials, and how to more fully develop your child's potential.

Also available: **How To Give Your Baby Encyclopedic Knowledge™ Video**
How To Give Your Baby Encyclopedic Knowledge™ Kits
How To Give Your Baby Encyclopedic Knowledge™ Audio Lectures

HOW TO MULTIPLY YOUR BABY'S INTELLIGENCE
Glenn Doman and Janet Doman

How To Multiply Your Baby's Intelligence provides a comprehensive program that will enable your child to read, do mathematics, and learn about anything and everything. It shows just how easy and pleasurable it is to teach your young child, and to help your child become more capable and confident. It explains how to begin and expand this remarkable program, how to make and organize your materials, and how to more fully develop your child's potential.

Also available: **How To Multiply Your Baby's Intelligence® Kits**

HOW TO TEACH YOUR BABY TO BE PHYSICALLY SUPERB
Glenn Doman, Douglas Doman, and Bruce Hagy

How To Teach Your Baby To Be Physically Superb explains the basic principles, philosophy, and stages of mobility in easy-to-understand language. This inspiring book describes just how easy and pleasurable it is to teach a young child to be physically superb. It clearly shows you how to create an environment for each stage of mobility that will help your baby advance and develop more easily. It shows that the team of mother, father, and baby is the most important athletic team your child will ever know. It explains how to begin, how to make your materials, and how to expand your program. This complete guide also includes full-color charts, photographs, illustrations, and detailed instructions to help you create your own program.

Also available: **How To Teach Your Baby To Be Physically Superb™ Video**
How To Teach Your Baby To Be Physically Superb™ Audio Lectures

WHAT TO DO ABOUT YOUR BRAIN-INJURED CHILD
Glenn Doman

In this breakthrough book, Glenn Doman—pioneer in the treatment of the brain-injured—brings real hope to thousands of children, many of whom are inoperable, and many of whom have been given up for lost and sentenced to a life of institutional confinement. Based upon the decades of successful work performed at The Institutes for the Achievement of Human Potential, the book explains why old theories and techniques fail, and why The Institutes philosophy and revolutionary treatment succeed.

CHILDREN'S BOOKS
About the Books

Very young readers have special needs. These are not met by conventional children's literature, which is designed to be read by adults to little children, not by them. The careful choice of vocabulary, sentence structure, print size, and formatting is needed by very young readers. The design of these children's books is based upon almost a half-century of search and discovery of what works best for very young readers.

ENOUGH, INIGO, ENOUGH
written by Janet Doman, illustrated by Michael Armentrout
Ages 1 to 6

NOSE IS NOT TOES
written by Glenn Doman, illustrated by Janet Doman
Ages 1 to 3

ENCYCLOPEDIC KNOWLEDGE SERIES
The Gentle Revolution Encyclopedic Knowledge Series includes the following *Bit of Intelligence* Sets:

A R T
Great Art Masterpieces
Self-Portraits of Great Artists
Masterpieces by da Vinci
Masterpieces by Picasso
Masterpieces by van Gogh

NATURAL HISTORY

Amphibians – Set I	Flowers
Primates – Set I	Insects
Birds	Leaves
Birds of Prey	Mammals
Butterflies and Moths	Reptiles
Dinosaurs	Sea Creatures

PEOPLE

Composers	Great Inventors
Explorers	World Leaders

Presidents of the United States – Set I

FOREIGN LANGUAGE

Basic Vocabulary in 10 Languages

MUSIC

Musical Instruments

ANATOMY

Organs of the Body

MATHEMATICS

Regular Polygons

P ɪ ᴄ ᴛ ᴜ ʀ ᴇ D ɪ ᴄ ᴛ ɪ ᴏ ɴ ᴀ ʀ ʏ
C D - R O M S

The Gentle Revolution Series includes ten volumes of the *Picture Dictionary CD-ROMs*.

The Picture Dictionary Program is designed to give parents a very easy-to-use method of introducing a program of encyclopedic knowledge in five different languages. A child may concentrate on a favorite language or gain ability in all five languages.

Each CD-ROM contains fifteen categories of Bit of Intelligence images, with ten images in each category. This is a total of 150 different images that can be viewed in English, Spanish, Japanese, Italian, and French on each CD-ROM.

For each image there is a large reading word provided. The child may choose to view the reading word alone, the image alone, or the reading word followed by the image. Mother and child may also create their own category by choosing images from the 150 images available on each CD-ROM.

This program is so easy to navigate that children as young as three years old have been able to use it independently.

*For information about these books
and teaching materials,
please contact:*

**The Gentle Revolution Press
810 Gleneagles Court, Suite 305
Towson, MD 21286 USA**

www.gentlerevolution.com

**PHONE: 410-337-5400
FAX: 410-337-3544
Toll-Free: 866-250-BABY
E-Mail: info@gentlerevolution.com**